NUMBER OPERATIONS

Subtraction

Second Edition

Illustrated by Laurie Conley, Gloria McKeown

Carol Gallivan
Ivy H. Greenburg
Alice R. Moss

ISBN 978-0-8454-6742-8

Copyright © 2010 The Continental Press, Inc.

No part of this publication may be reproduced in any form or by any means, electronic, mechanical, photocopying, recording, or otherwise, without the prior written permission of the publisher. All rights reserved. Printed in the United States of America.

CONTENTS

Subtracting Sets—Teaching Page	3
Subtracting Sets	4
Minus Sign—Teaching Page	5
Minus Sign	6
Subtraction Facts—Teaching Page	7
Subtract 1	8
Subtract 1	9
Subtract 1	10
Subtract 1—Review	11
Subtract 2	12
Subtract 2	13
Subtract 2	14
Subtract 3	15
Subtract 3	16
Subtract 4	17
Subtract 1–4—Review	18
Subtract 1–4—Review	19
Subtract Equal Numbers—Teaching Page	20
Subtract Equal Numbers	21
Subtract Equal Numbers	22
Subtract Equal Numbers	23
Subtract Equal Numbers	24
Subtract 1–5—Review	25
Subtract 0—Teaching Page	26
Subtract 0	27
Subtract 0	28
Subtract 0	29
Subtract 0	30
Subtract 0–5—Review	31
Subtract from 6	32
Subtract from 6	33
Subtract from 6	34
Subtract from 6	35
Subtract from 6	36
Subtract from 1–6—Review	37
Subtract from 7	38
Subtract from 7	39
Subtract from 7	40
Subtract from 7	41
Subtract from 7	42
Subtract from 7	43
Subtract from 1–7—Review	44
Subtract from 1–7—Review	45
Subtract from 8	46
Subtract from 8	47
Subtract from 8	48
Subtract from 8	49
Subtract from 8	50
Subtract from 8	51
Subtract from 8	52
Subtract from 1–8—Review	53
Subtract from 1–8—Review	54
Subtract from 9	55
Subtract from 9	56
Subtract from 9	57
Subtract from 9	58
Subtract from 9	59
Subtract from 9	60
Subtract from 9	61
Subtract from 9	62
Subtract from 1–9—Review	63
Subtract from 1–9—Review	64
Word Problems—Teaching Page	65
Subtract from 10	66
Subtract from 10	67
Subtract from 10	68
Subtract from 10	69
Subtract from 10	70
Subtract from 10	71
Subtract from 10	72
Subtract from 10	73
Subtract from 10	74
Subtract from 1–10—Review	75
Subtract from 1–10—Review	76
Word Problems	77
Subtract Equal Numbers	78
Subtract Equal Numbers	79
Subtract Equal Numbers	80
Subtract Equal Numbers	81
Subtract Equal Numbers	82
Subtract 0	83
Subtract 0	84
Subtract 0	85
Subtract 0	86
Subtract 0	87
Subtract 0–10—Review	88
Subtract 0–10—Review	89
Subtract 0–10—Review	90
Subtract 0–10—Review	91
Word Problems	92
Pretest/Posttest	T-1
Pretest/Posttest	T-2
Pretest/Posttest	T-3
Pretest/Posttest	T-4

Subtract to take away. Look at the set. Take away a number of objects. Then you have a new set with the objects that are left.

There are 2 clouds in the set below. The problem says to take away 1. Cross out 1 cloud. There is 1 cloud that is not crossed out. So, there is 1 cloud left.

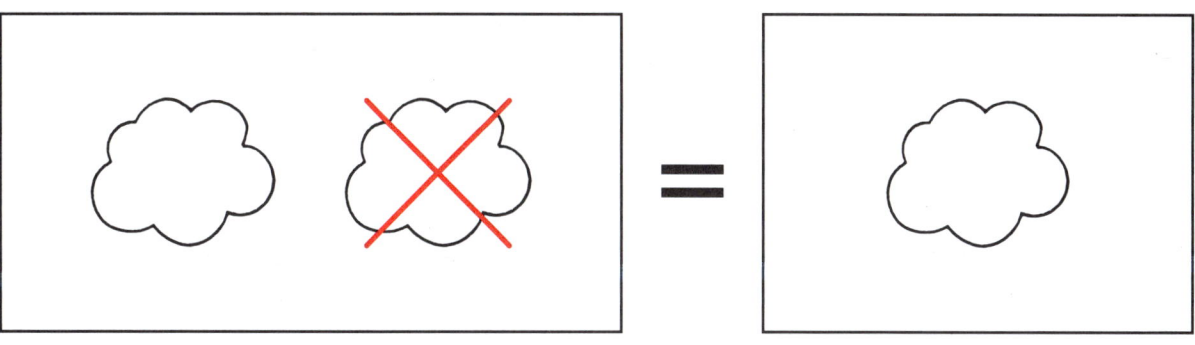

2   take away   1   =   1

There are 3 moons in the set below. The problem says to take away 1. Cross out 1 moon. How many moons are not crossed out? There are 2 moons left.

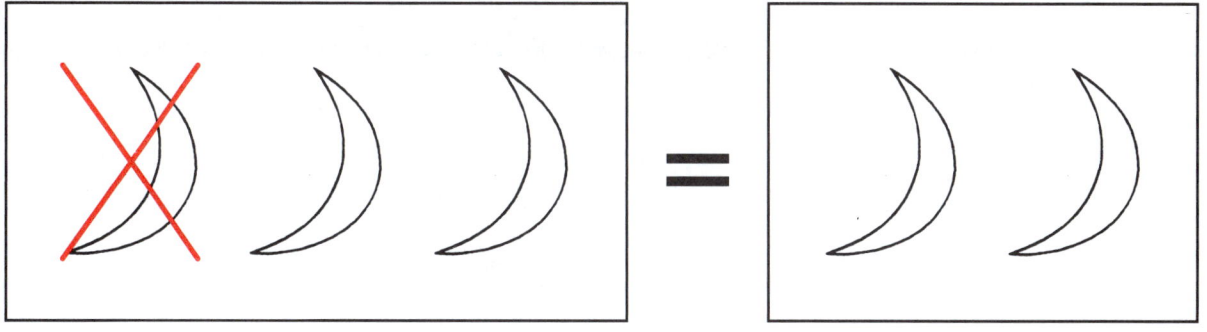

3   take away   1   =   2

Subtracting Sets—Teaching Page

Draw and write the answer.

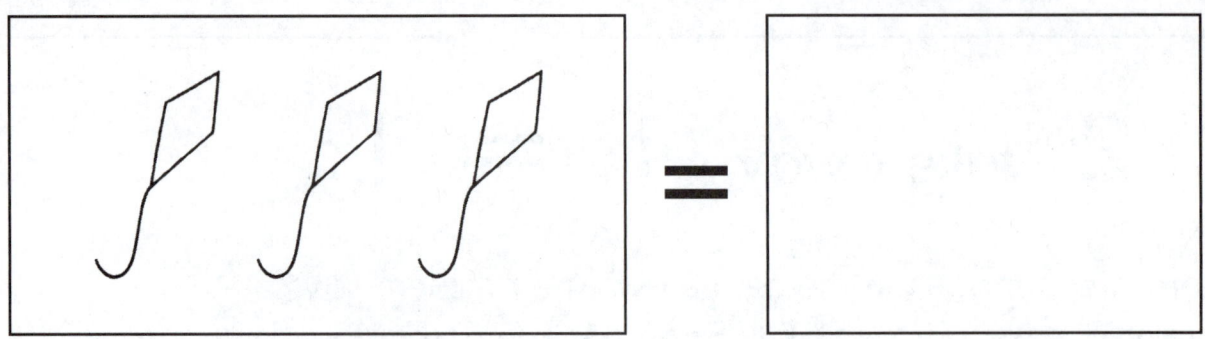

3   take away   1   =   _____

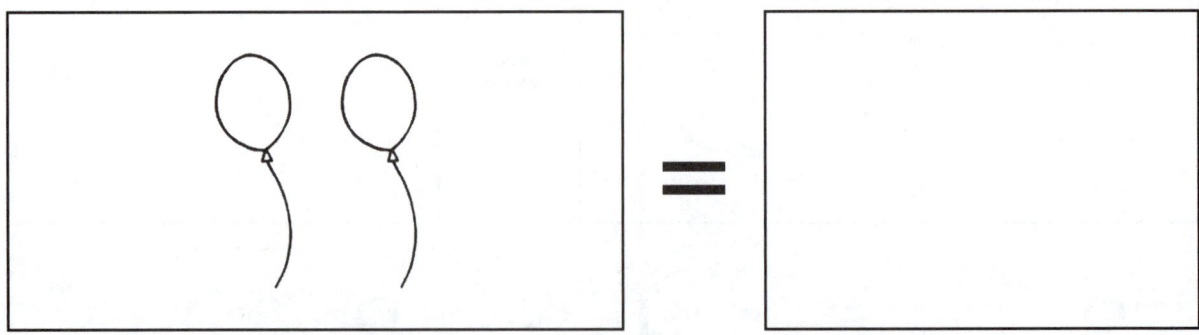

3   take away   1   =   _____

2   take away   1   =   _____

4 Subtracting Sets

© The Continental Press, Inc.
DUPLICATING THIS MATERIAL IS ILLEGAL.

There is a special sign to show subtraction. The sign looks like this: —. It is called a **minus sign.**

The problem below shows subtraction. There are 2 horses. Then 1 horse is taken away. So there is 1 horse left. Use the minus sign and the equals sign to show the subtraction.

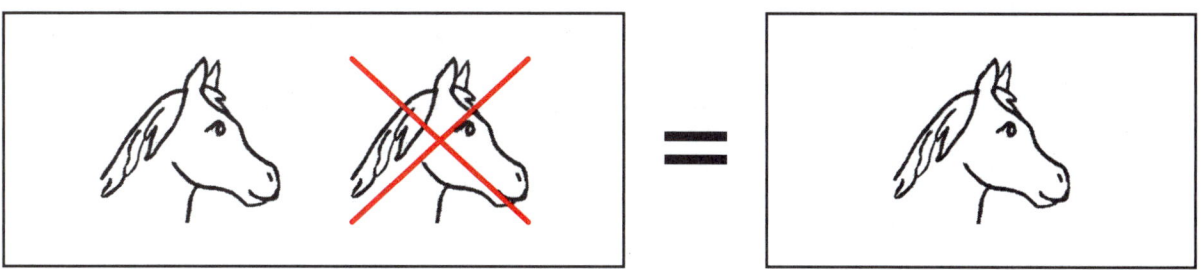

2 — 1 = 1

You can say, "2 horses minus 1 horse equals 1 horse."

Look at the problem below. It shows subtraction. Write a — sign.

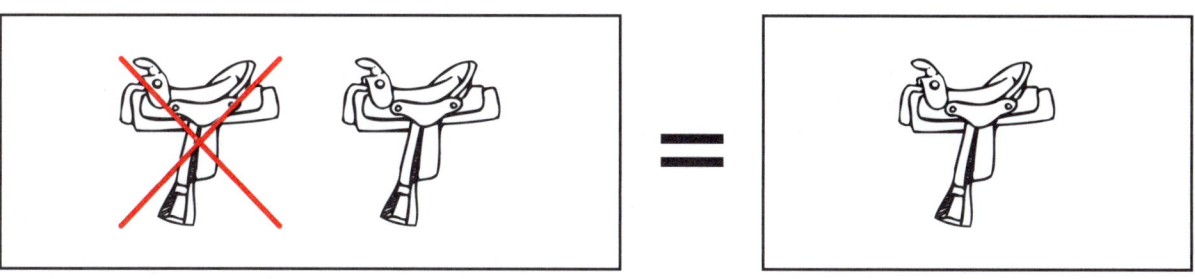

2 ⋯ 1 = 1

Write a — sign.

· · · · ·   · · · · ·   · · · · ·   · · · · ·   · · · · ·

· · · · ·   · · · · ·   · · · · ·   · · · · ·   · · · · ·

Minus Sign—Teaching Page

Write a − sign.

3 .... 1 = 2

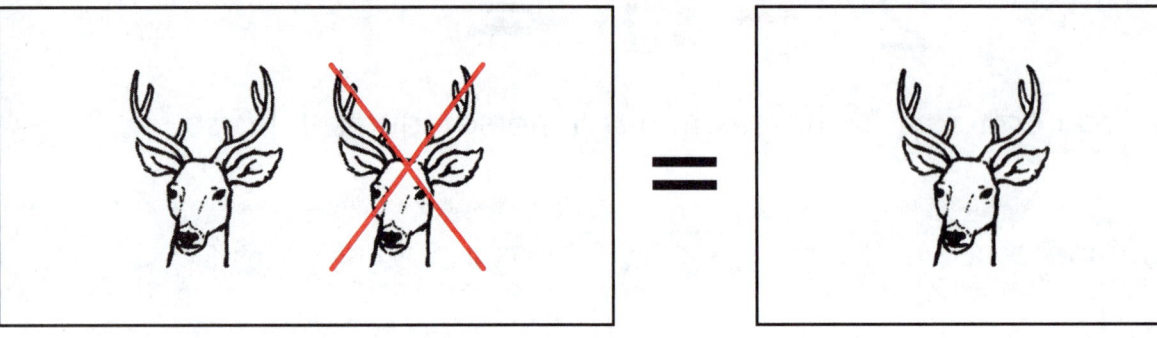

2   I   =   I

Write a − sign. Write an = sign.

3   I   2
---
2   I   I

6 Minus Sign

Subtract to take a group apart.

Use numbers and signs to write a subtraction fact.

You can write subtraction facts two different ways.

You can write them across.

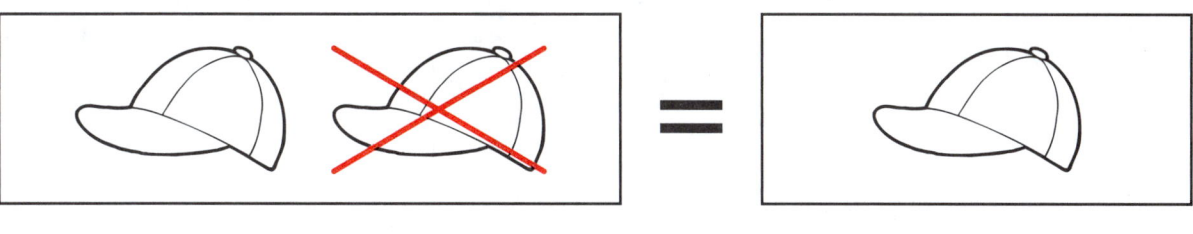

2 − 1 = 1

You can write them up and down.

Subtract.

2 − 1 = ___

3 − 1 = ___

$\begin{array}{r} 2 \\ -1 \\ \hline \end{array}$ $\begin{array}{r} 3 \\ -1 \\ \hline \end{array}$

Subtraction Facts—Teaching Page   **7**

Subtract.

3 − 1 = ____

$$\begin{array}{r} 2 \\ -\ 1 \\ \hline \square \end{array}$$

2 − 1 = ____

3 − 1 = ____

$$\begin{array}{r} 2 \\ -\ 1 \\ \hline \square \end{array} \qquad \begin{array}{r} 3 \\ -\ 1 \\ \hline \square \end{array}$$

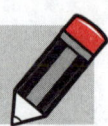

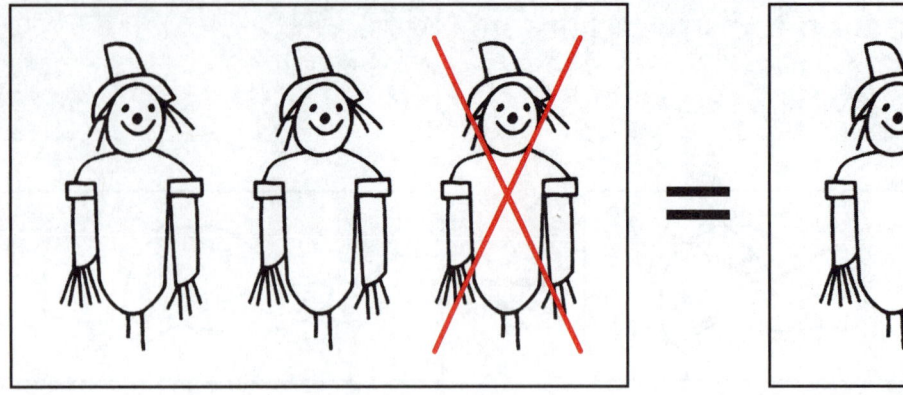

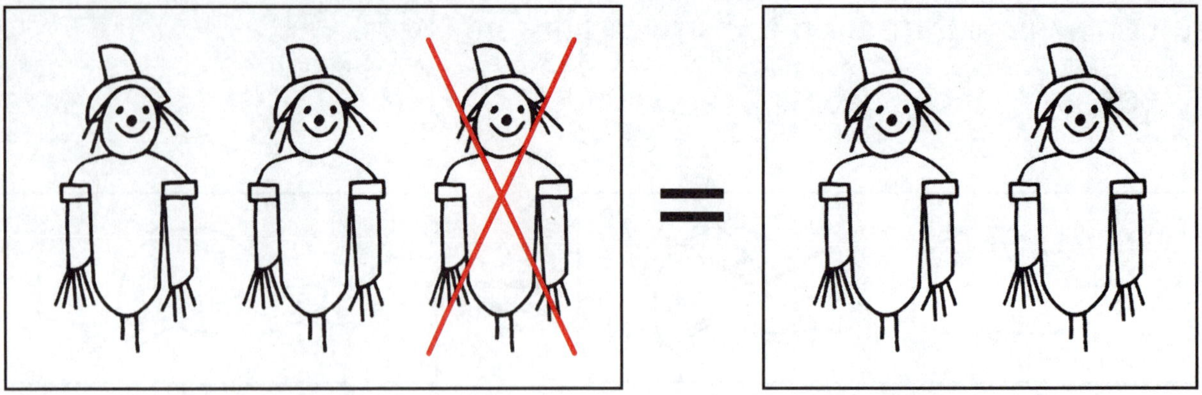

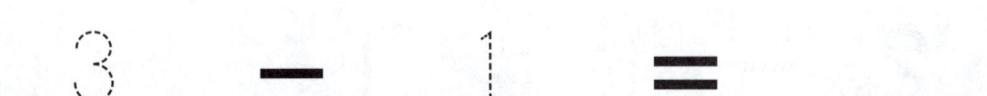

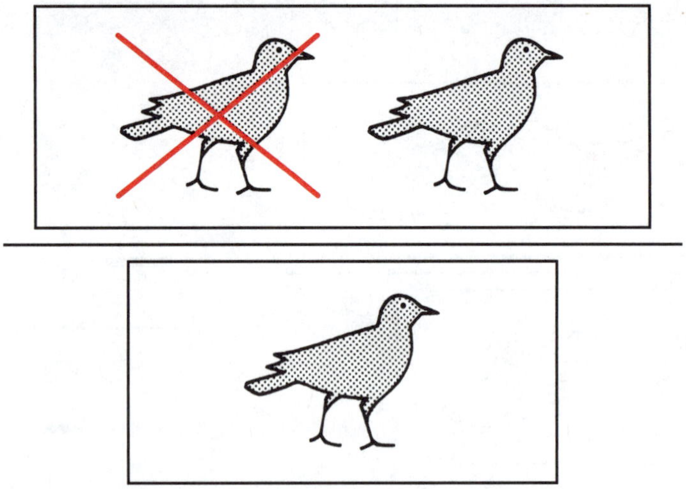

Subtract.

4 − 1 = ____

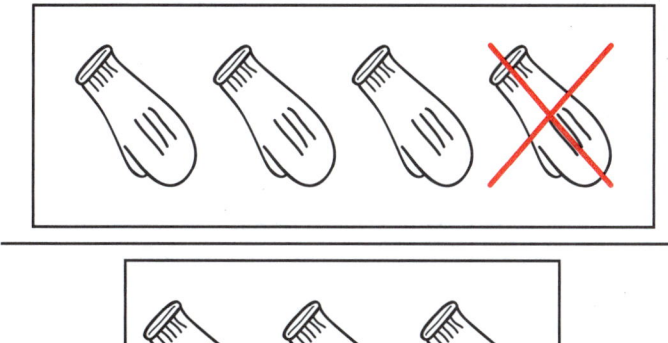 

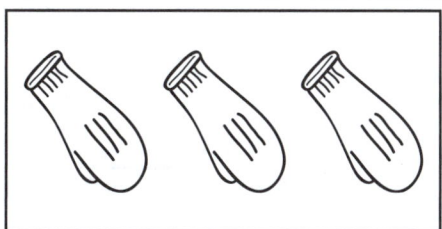

4 − 1 = ____

4 − 1 = ____

4
−1
____

4
−1
____

Subtract 1

Subtract.

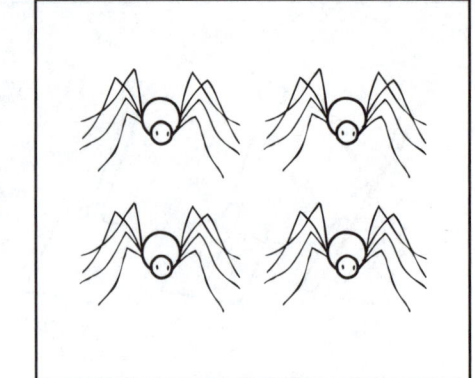

5   -   1   =   ___

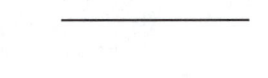

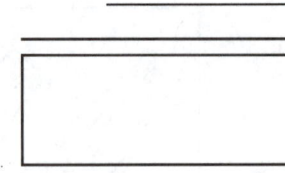

5 - 1 = ___

5 - 1 = ___

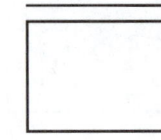

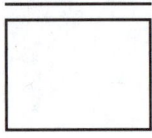

10   Subtract 1

Cross out the squares.
Then write the answer.

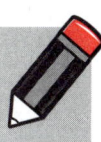

$$\begin{array}{r} 2 \\ -1 \\ \hline \end{array}$$

□ ☒

$$\begin{array}{r} 3 \\ -1 \\ \hline \end{array}$$

□ □ □

□ □ □ □ □

$5 - 1 =$

□ □ □ □

$4 - 1 =$

Subtract.

$$\begin{array}{r} 4 \\ -1 \\ \hline \end{array}$$

$$\begin{array}{r} 5 \\ -1 \\ \hline \end{array}$$

$3 - 1 =$

$2 - 1 =$

$5 - 1 =$

$4 - 1 =$

Subtract.

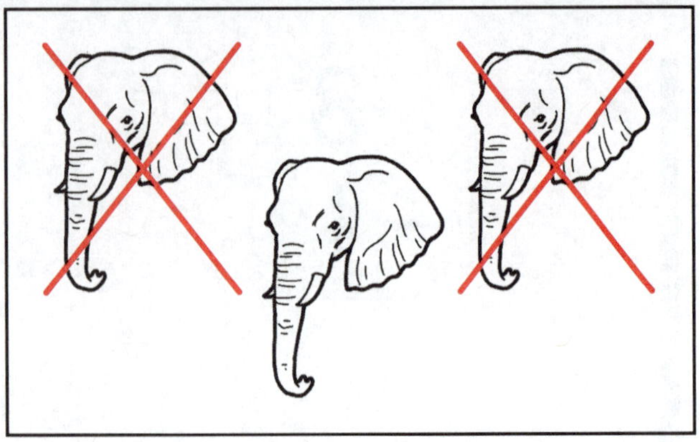

3 − 2 = ___

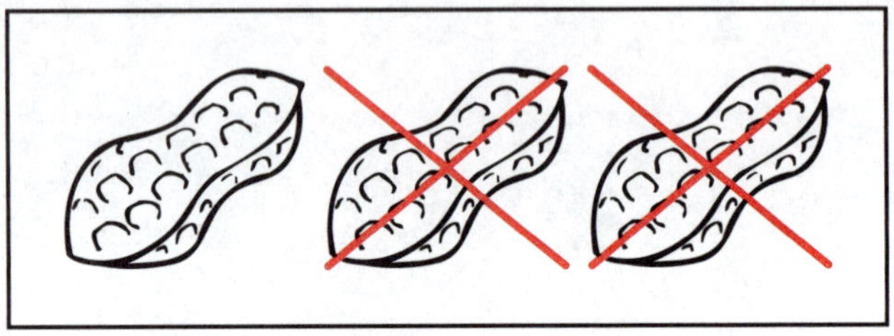

3 − 2 = ___

3 − 2 = ___

$\begin{array}{r}3\\-2\\\hline\end{array}$ $\begin{array}{r}3\\-2\\\hline\end{array}$

12   Subtract 2

Subtract.

_4_ − _2_ = ___

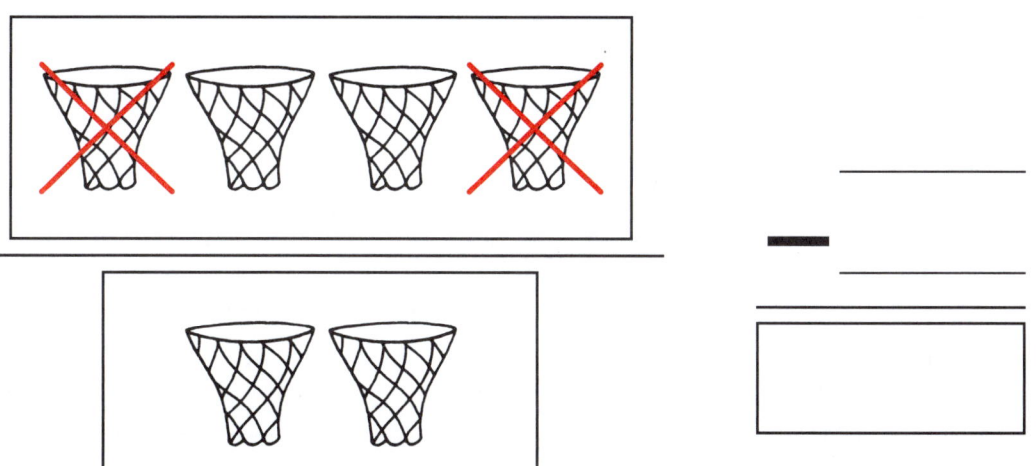

4 − 2 = ___

4 − 2 = ___

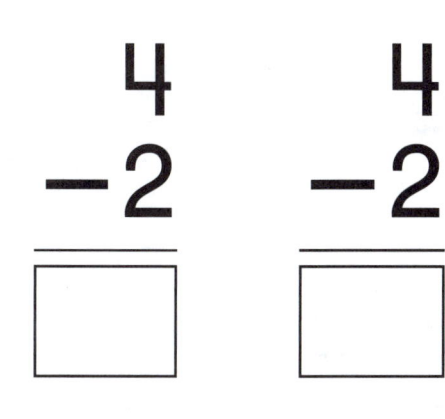

Subtract 2   **13**

Subtract.

=

5 – 2 = ____

____
– ____
____

$5 - 2 =$ ____

$5 - 2 =$ ____

$$\begin{array}{r} 5 \\ -2 \\ \hline \square \end{array} \qquad \begin{array}{r} 5 \\ -2 \\ \hline \square \end{array}$$

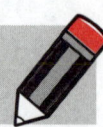

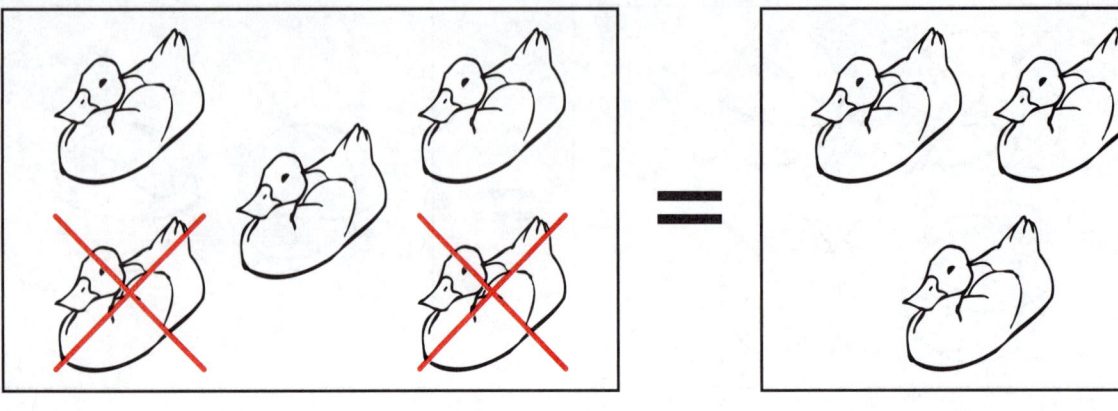

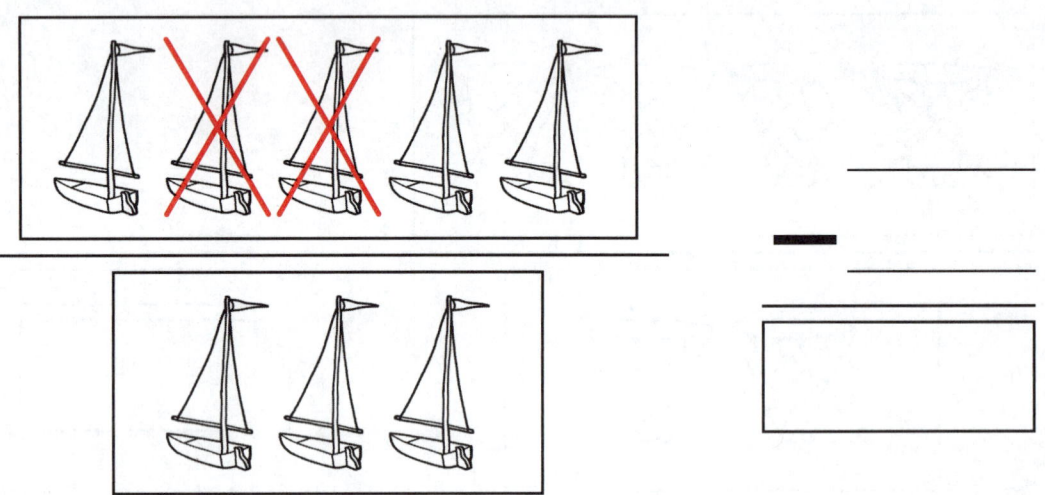

Subtract.

4 − 3 = _____

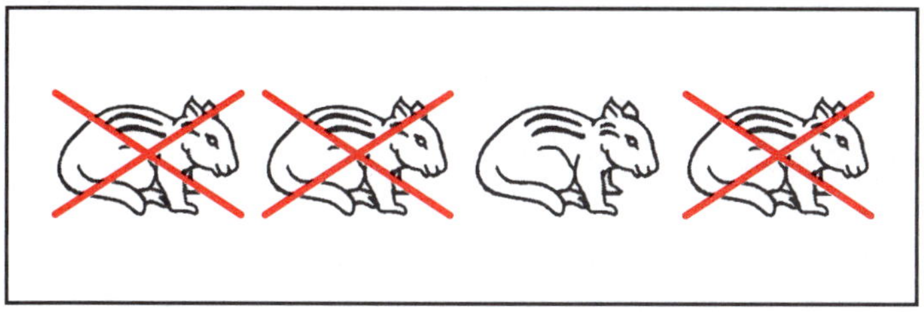

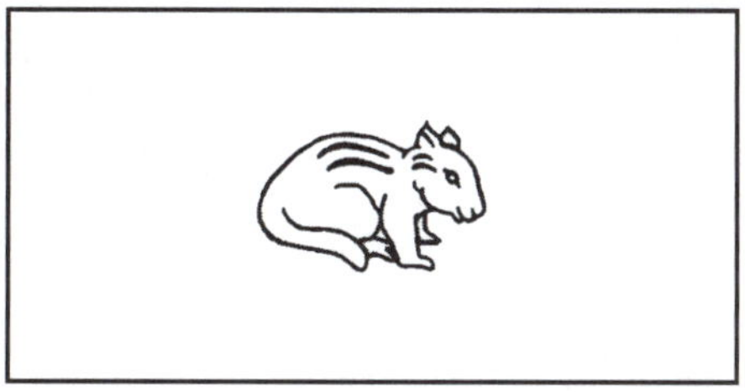

_____
− _____
_____

4 − 3 = _____

4 − 3 = _____

4
−3
___

4
−3
___

Subtract 3   **15**

Subtract.

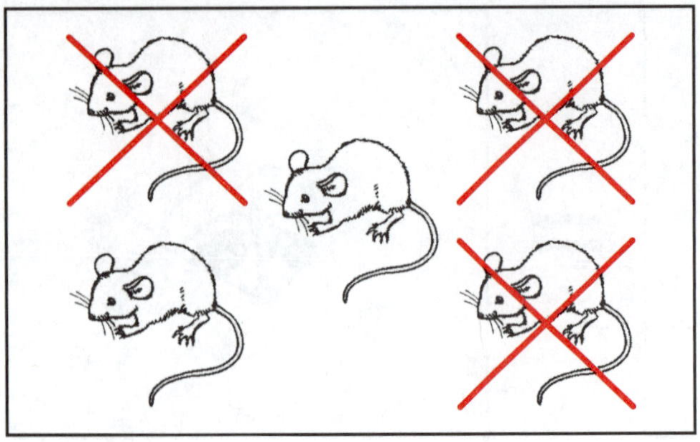

___5___ − ___3___ = _____

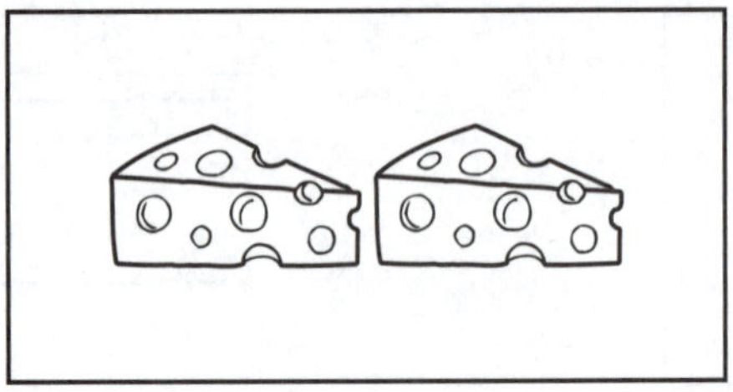

5 − 3 = _____

5 − 3 = _____

$\begin{array}{r}5\\-3\\\hline\end{array}$ $\begin{array}{r}5\\-3\\\hline\end{array}$

16   Subtract 3

© The Continental Press, Inc.
DUPLICATING THIS MATERIAL IS ILLEGAL.

Subtract.

5 − 4 = ___

 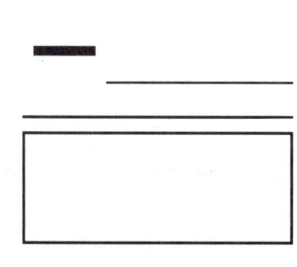

5 − 4 = ___

5 − 4 = ___

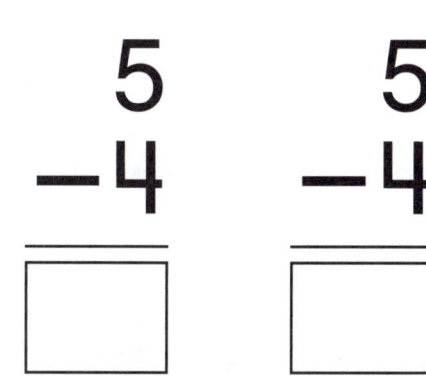

Subtract 4 **17**

Cross out the squares.
Then write the answer.

☐☐☐☐
4 − 3 =

☐☐☐☐☐
5 − 4 =

4 ☐☐☐☐
−2
___

5 ☐☐☐☐☐
−3
___

☐☐☐
3 − 1 =

☐☐
2 − 1 =

5 ☐☐☐☐☐
−1
___

3 ☐☐☐
−2
___

☐☐☐☐☐
5 − 2 =

☐☐☐☐
4 − 1 =

18 Subtract 1–4—Review

Subtract.

3 − 2 =	4 − 3 =
4 −1	5 −2
3 − 1 =	5 − 3 =
5 −4	2 −1
4 − 2 =	5 − 1 =

Subtract 1–4—Review

Equal numbers are the same. When you subtract equal numbers, the answer is always 0.

Look at the problem below. There is 1 airplane. Take away 1 airplane. There are 0 airplanes left.

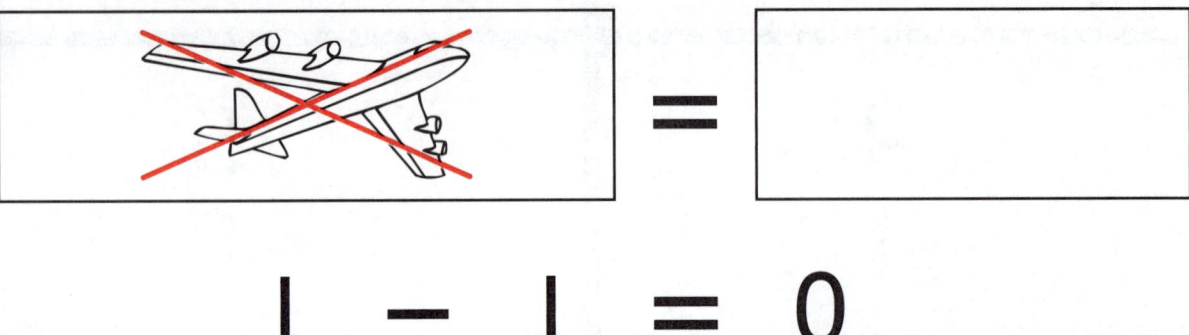

1 − 1 = 0

Look at the problem below. There are 2 buses. Take away 2 buses. There are 0 buses left.

$$\begin{array}{r}2\\-2\\\hline 0\end{array}$$

Subtract.

1 − 1 = ___

2 − 2 = ___

$$\begin{array}{r}1\\-1\\\hline\end{array}$$

$$\begin{array}{r}2\\-2\\\hline\end{array}$$

Subtract.

2 − 2 = ___

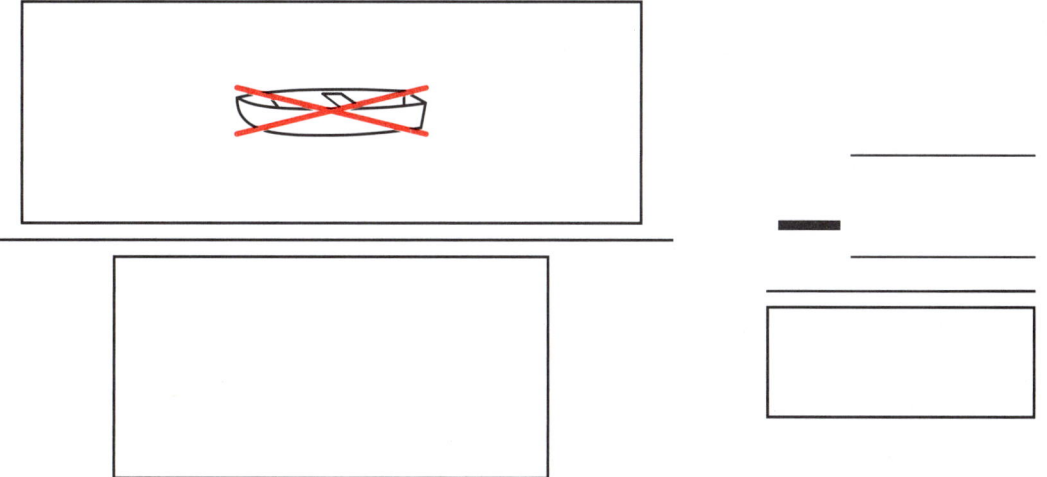

1 − 1 = ___

2 − 2 = ___

  1
−1
___

  2
−2
___

Subtract Equal Numbers

Subtract.

_3_ − _3_ = ___

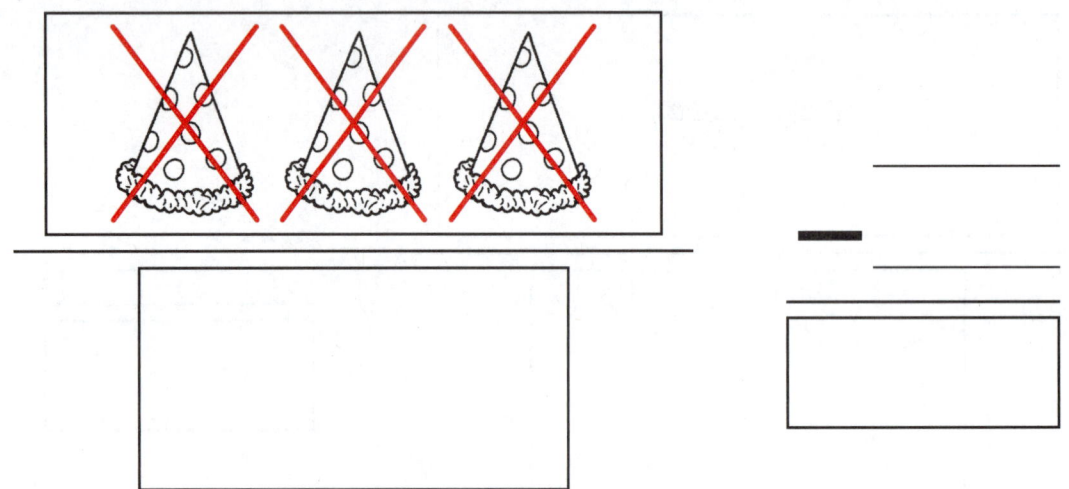

3 − 3 = ___

3 − 3 = ___

```
  3        3
− 3      − 3
────     ────
```

22 Subtract Equal Numbers

Subtract.

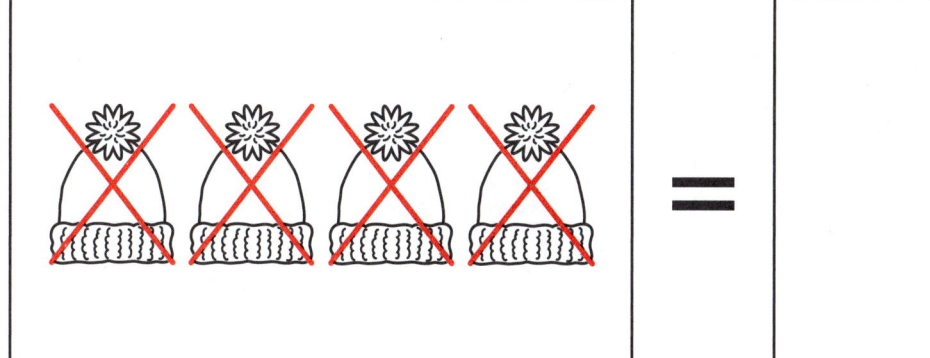

4 − 4 = ___

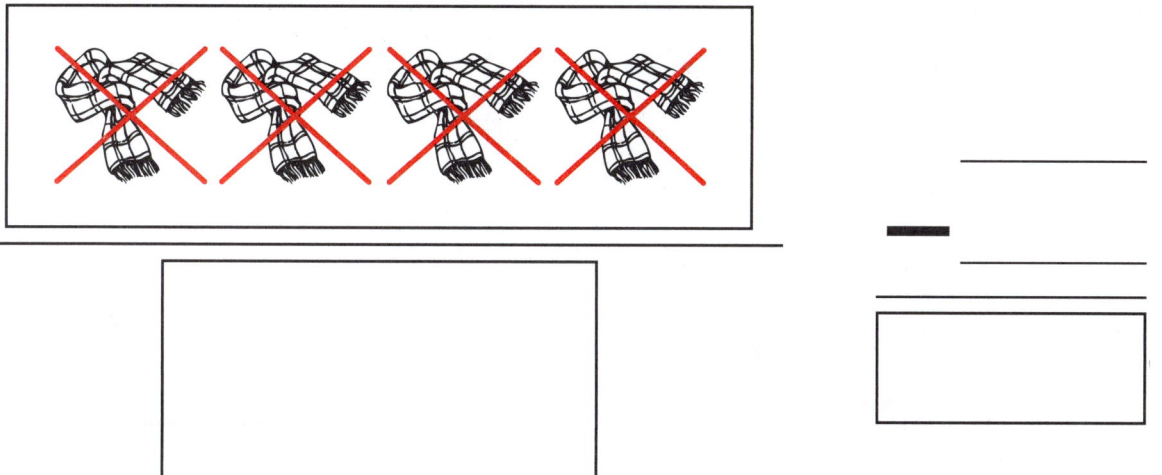

4 − 4 = ___

4 − 4 = ___

$$\begin{array}{r}4\\-4\\\hline\end{array}$$ $$\begin{array}{r}4\\-4\\\hline\end{array}$$

Subtract Equal Numbers **23**

Subtract.

___5___ − ___5___ = _____

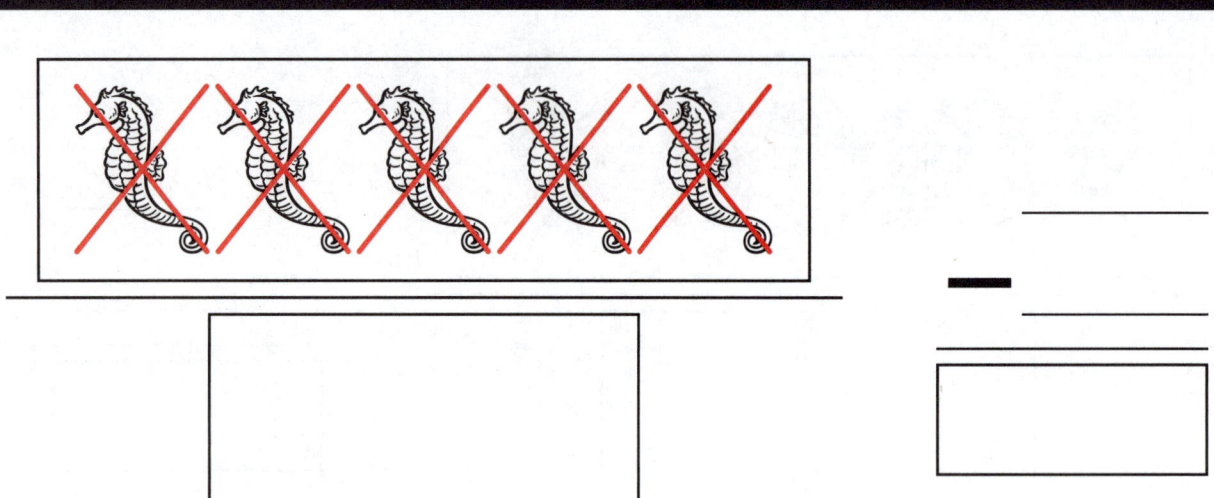

5 − 5 = _____

5 − 5 = _____

```
   5        5
  −5       −5
  ──       ──
```

24 Subtract Equal Numbers

Cross out the squares.
Then write the answer.

2 □□
−2
___

4 □□□□
−4
___

□□□□
4 − 2 =

□□□□
5 − 5 =

Subtract.

3
−3
___

5
−2
___

5 − 4 =

4 − 3 =

3 − 2 =

1 − 1 =

Subtract 1–5—Review   **25**

Subtract 0 from a number. The number does not change. The answer is always the same number.

Look at the problem below. There is 1 snake. Take away 0 snakes. There is 1 snake left.

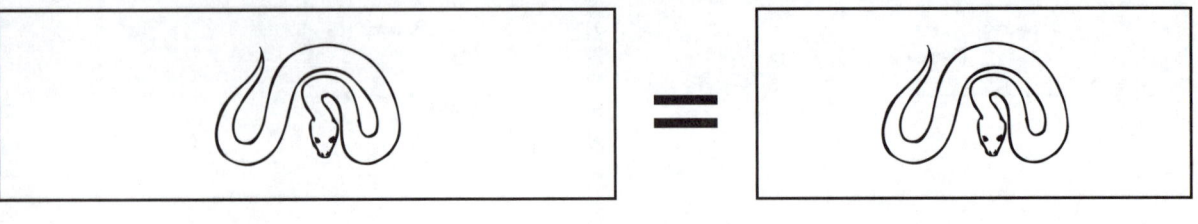

$1 - 0 = 1$

Look at the problem below. There are 2 turtles. Take away 0 turtles. There are 2 turtles left.

$$\begin{array}{r} 2 \\ -0 \\ \hline 2 \end{array}$$

Subtract.

$1 - 0 = $ ____

$2 - 0 = $ ____

$$\begin{array}{r} 1 \\ -0 \\ \hline \end{array} \qquad \begin{array}{r} 2 \\ -0 \\ \hline \end{array}$$

26 Subtract 0—Teaching Page

© The Continental Press, Inc.
DUPLICATING THIS MATERIAL IS ILLEGAL.

Subtract.

2 − 0 = ___

1 − 0 = ___

2 − 0 = ___

$\begin{array}{r}1\\-0\\\hline\end{array}$ $\begin{array}{r}2\\-0\\\hline\end{array}$

Subtract.

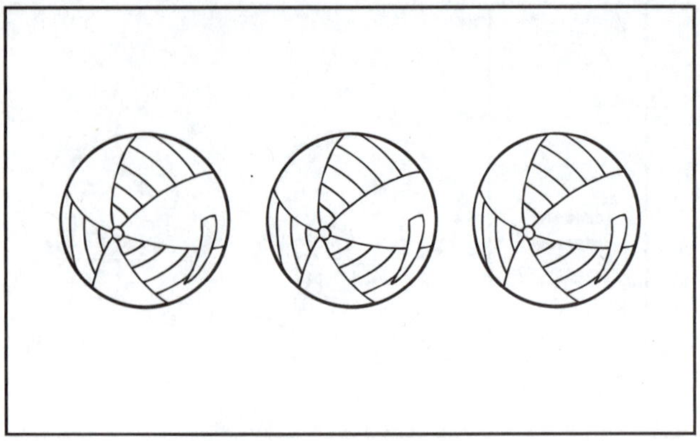

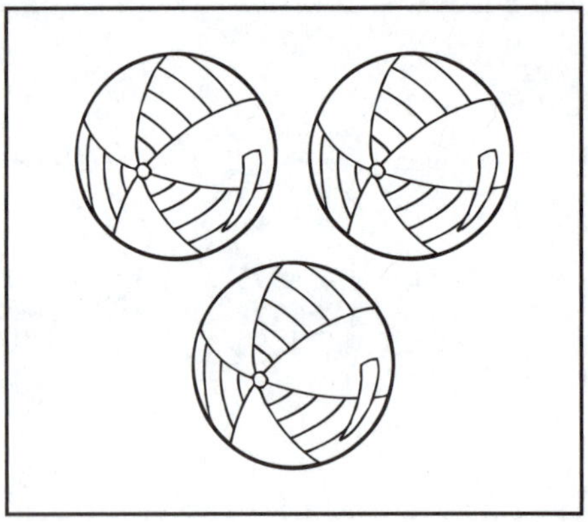

3 − 0 = ___

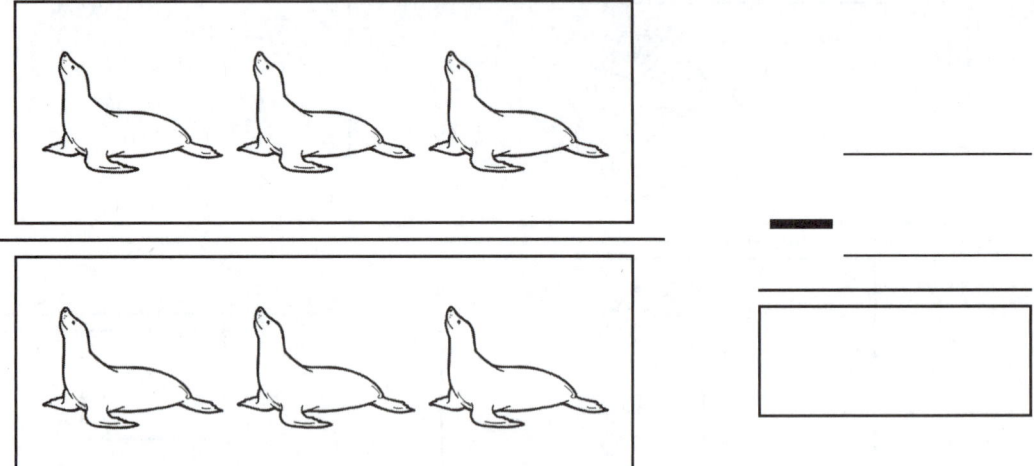

3 − 0 = ___

3 − 0 = ___

3
−0
___

3
−0
___

28   Subtract 0

Subtract.

4 − 0 = ___

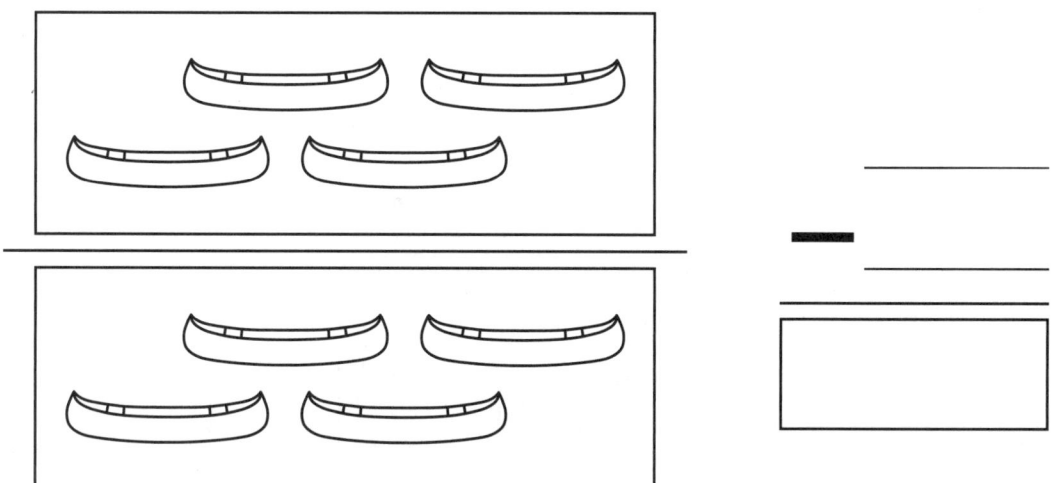

4 − 0 = ___

4 − 0 = ___

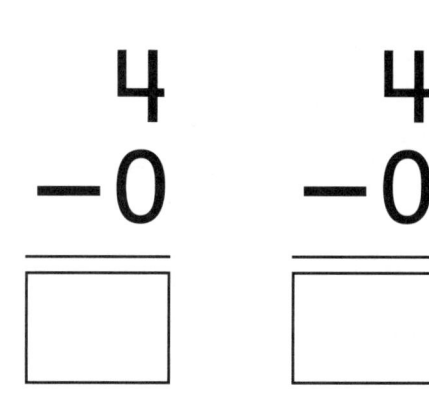

Subtract 0   29

Subtract.

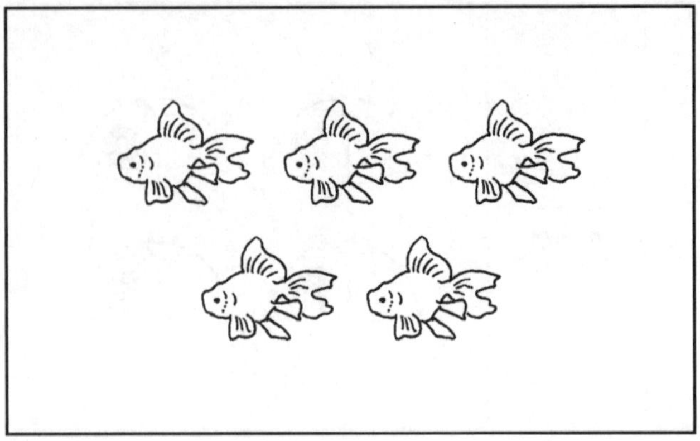

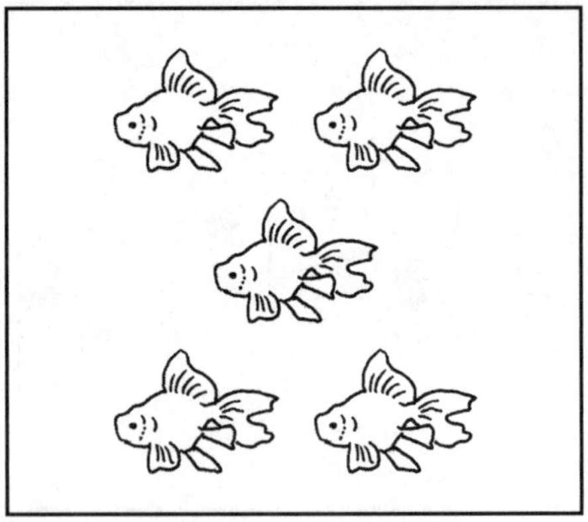

5 − 0 = ____

5 − 0 = ____

5 − 0 = ____

   5   5
 −0   −0

30 Subtract 0

**Cross out the squares.
Then write the answer.**

5 ☐☐☐☐☐
−4
___

4 ☐☐☐☐
−4
___

☐
1 − 0 =

☐☐☐☐☐
5 − 0 =

Subtract.

5
−3
___

3
−0
___

4 − 0 =

1 − 1 =

4 − 2 =

2 − 0 =

© The Continental Press, Inc.
DUPLICATING THIS MATERIAL IS ILLEGAL.

Subtract 0–5—Review **31**

Subtract.

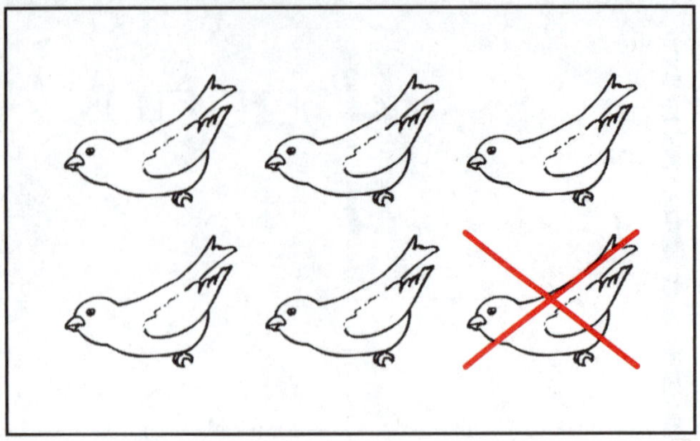

6 − 1 = ___

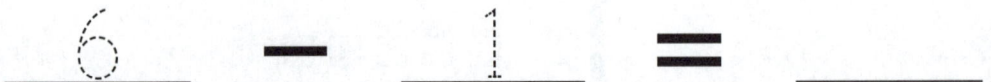

6 − 1 = ___

6 − 1 = ___

6
−1
___

6
−1
___

32 Subtract from 6

Subtract.

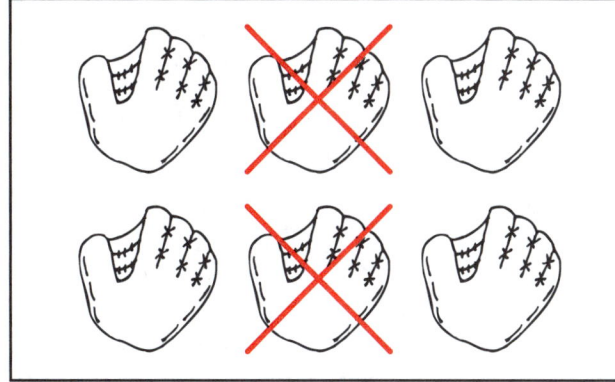 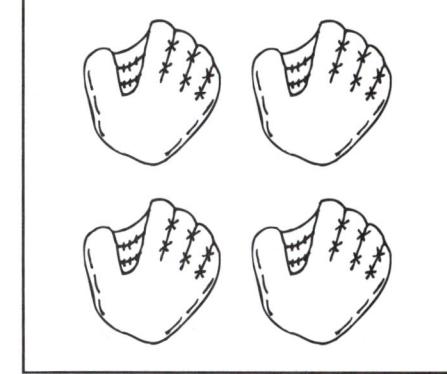

___6___ − ___2___ = _____

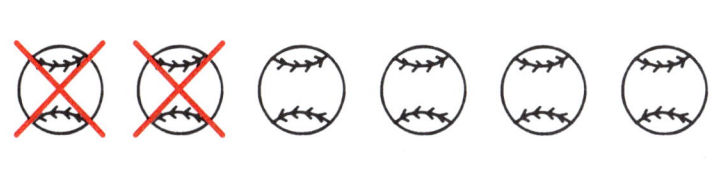

6 − 2 = _____

6 − 2 = _____

$\begin{array}{r}6\\-2\\\hline\end{array}$ $\begin{array}{r}6\\-2\\\hline\end{array}$

Subtract from 6 **33**

Subtract.

=

6 – 3 = ____

$$\begin{array}{r} ___ \\ -\ ___ \\ \hline \square \end{array}$$

6 – 3 = ____

6 – 3 = ____

$$\begin{array}{r} 6 \\ -3 \\ \hline \square \end{array} \qquad \begin{array}{r} 6 \\ -3 \\ \hline \square \end{array}$$

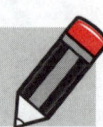

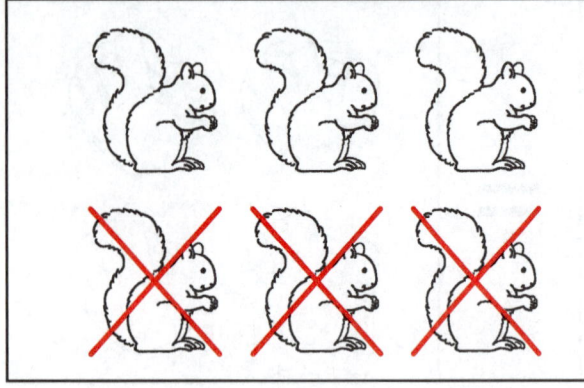

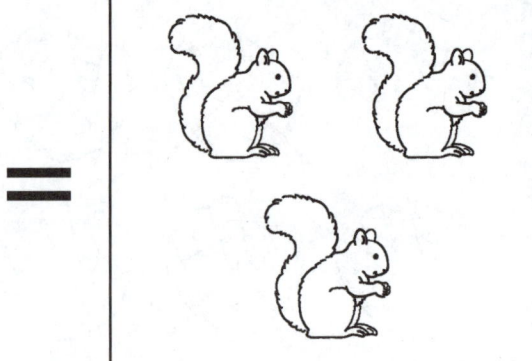

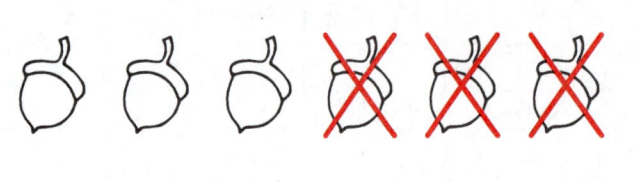

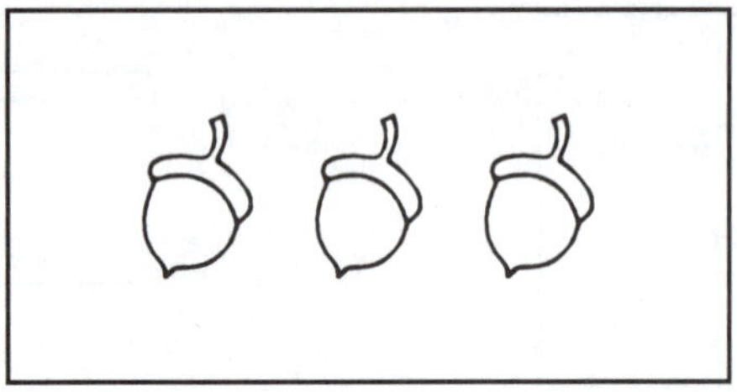

Subtract.

6 − 4 = ____

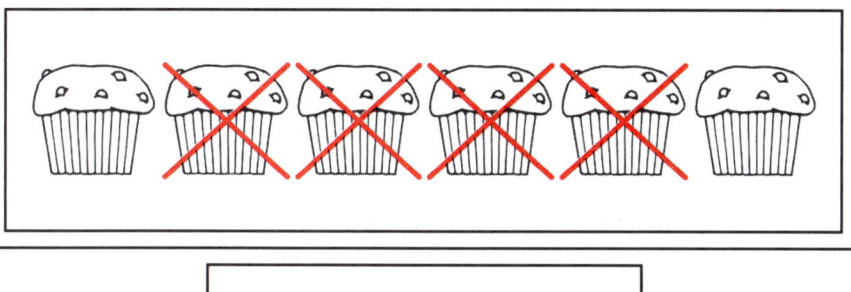

6 − 4 = ____

6 − 4 = ____

$$\begin{array}{r}6\\-4\\\hline\end{array}$$ $$\begin{array}{r}6\\-4\\\hline\end{array}$$

Subtract from 6   **35**

Subtract.

 =

6 − 5 = ___

   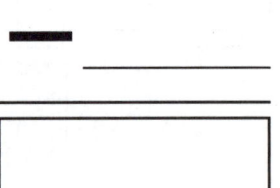

6 − 5 = ___

6 − 5 = ___

```
  6      6
 −5     −5
 ☐      ☐
```

36   Subtract from 6

Cross out the squares.
Then write the answer.

☐☐☐☐
6 ☐
−4
___

1 ☐
−0
___

☐☐☐☐
☐
6 − 1 =

☐☐☐☐
☐
6 − 5 =

Subtract.

2
−2
___

6
−2
___

5 − 4 =

3 − 1 =

6 − 3 =

4 − 2 =

Subtract from 1–6—Review   37

Subtract.

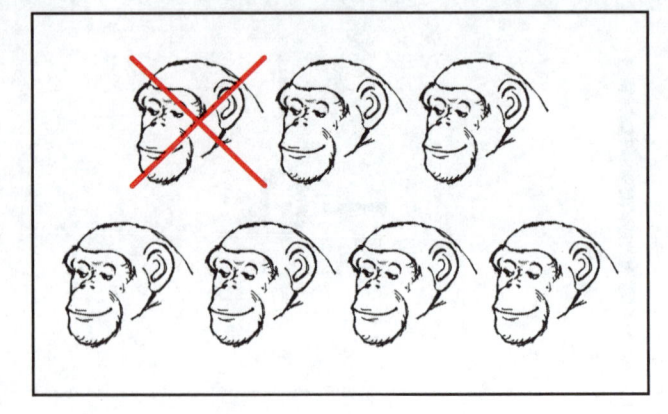

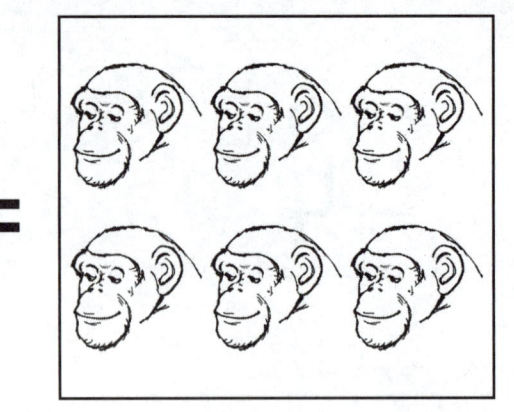

7 − 1 = ___

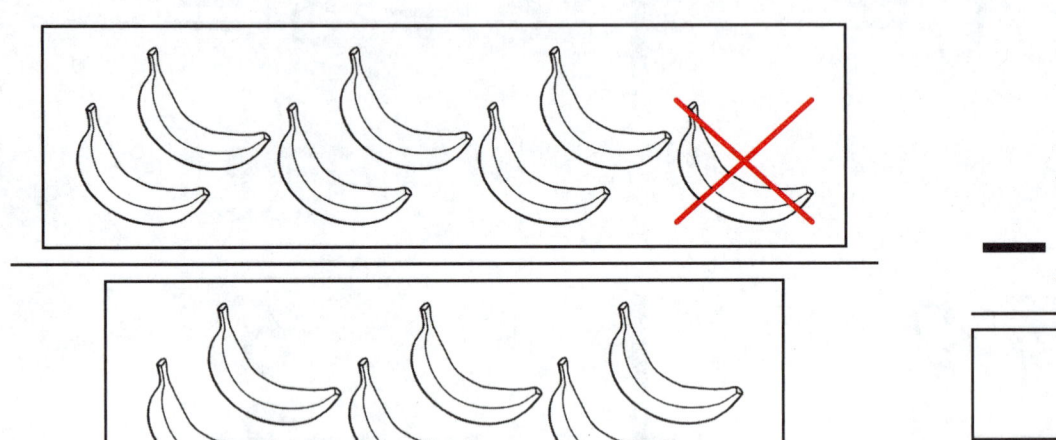

7 − 1 = ___

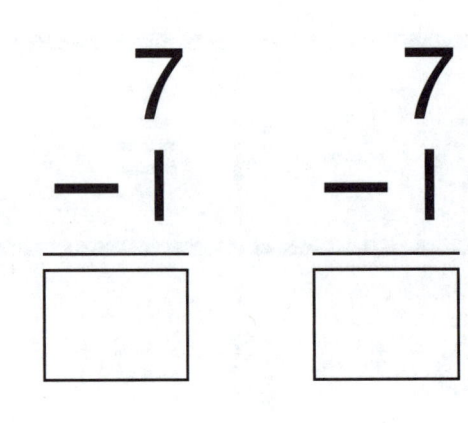

7 − 1 = ___

7
−1
☐

7
−1
☐

38 Subtract from 7

Subtract.

_7_ − _2_ = _____

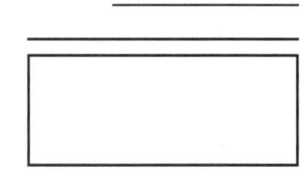

7 − 2 = _____

7 − 2 = _____

7
−2
___

7
−2
___

Subtract from 7   **39**

Subtract.

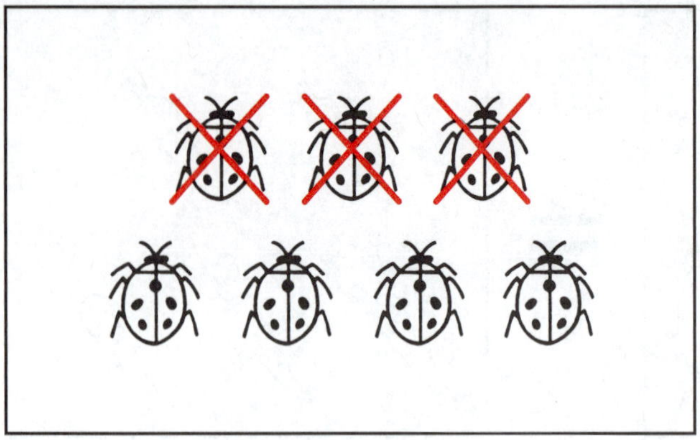

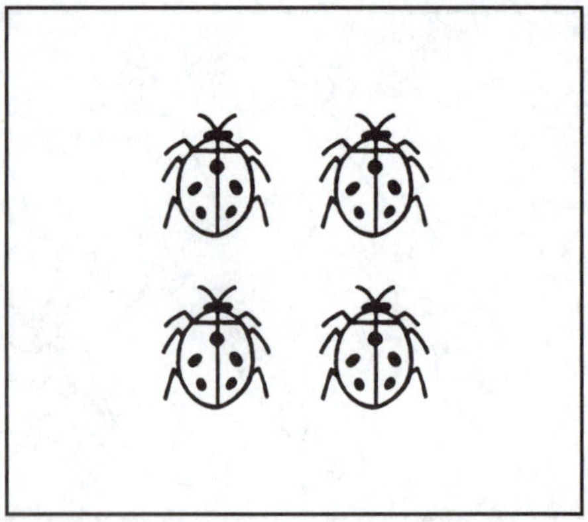

_7_ − _3_ = ____

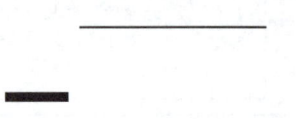

40   Subtract from 7

Subtract.

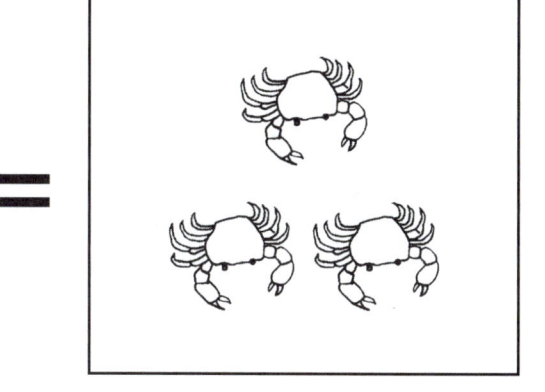

7 − 4 = ___

7 − 4 = ___

7 − 4 = ___

$$\begin{array}{r}7\\-4\\\hline\end{array}\qquad\begin{array}{r}7\\-4\\\hline\end{array}$$

Subtract from 7   **41**

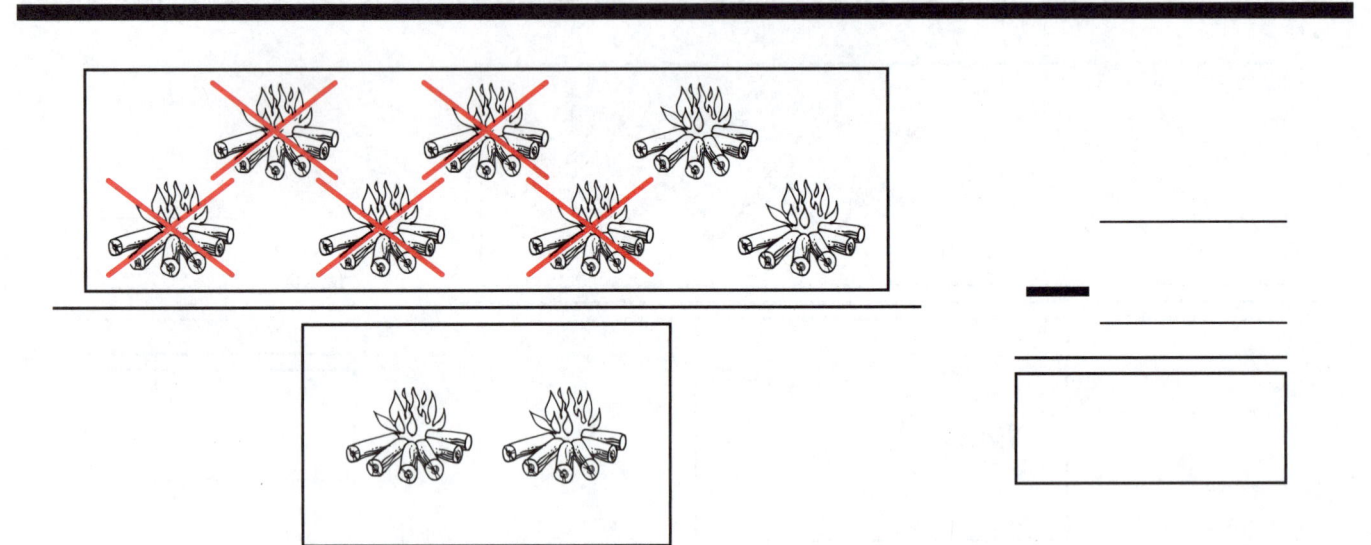

Subtract.

7 − 5 = ___

7 − 5 = ___

7 − 5 = ___

$$\begin{array}{r}7\\-5\\\hline\end{array}\qquad\begin{array}{r}7\\-5\\\hline\end{array}$$

42   Subtract from 7

Subtract.

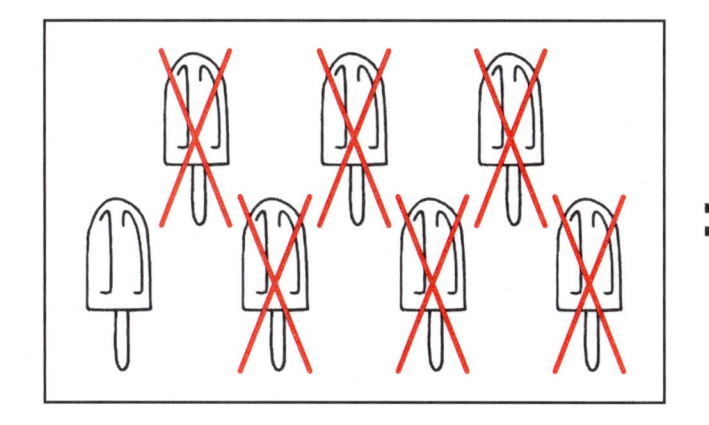

_7_ − _6_ = ___

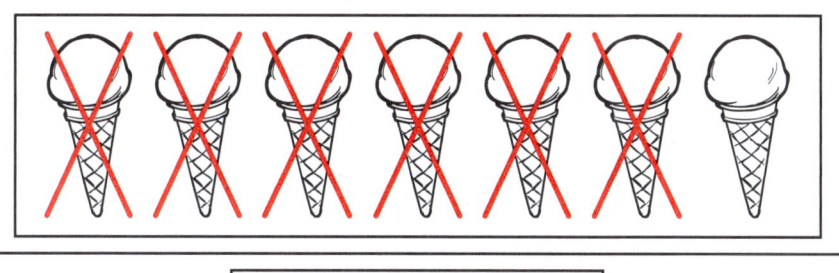

7 − 6 = ___

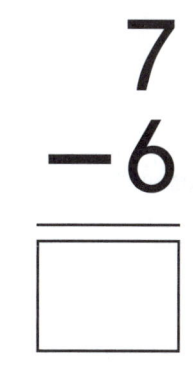

7 − 6 = ___

7
−6
___

7
−6
___

Subtract from 7   **43**

Cross out the squares.
Then write the answer.

☐☐☐☐☐
☐☐
7 − 5 =

☐☐☐☐☐
☐☐
7 − 4 =

7 ☐☐☐☐☐
☐☐
−3
___

4 ☐☐☐☐
−3
___

☐☐☐☐☐
☐☐
7 − 6 =

☐
1 − 1 =

2 ☐☐
−0
___

7 ☐☐☐☐☐
☐☐
−2
___

☐☐☐☐☐
5 − 2 =

☐☐☐
3 − 1 =

44   Subtract from 1–7—Review

Subtract.

7 − 3 =	6 − 4 =
6 −3	1 −0
5 − 5 =	4 − 1 =
6 −5	7 −4
7 − 5 =	5 − 3 =

Subtract from 1–7 — Review

Subtract.

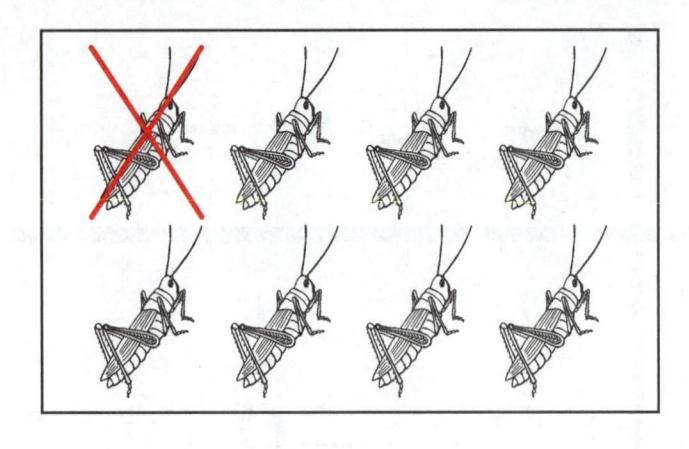

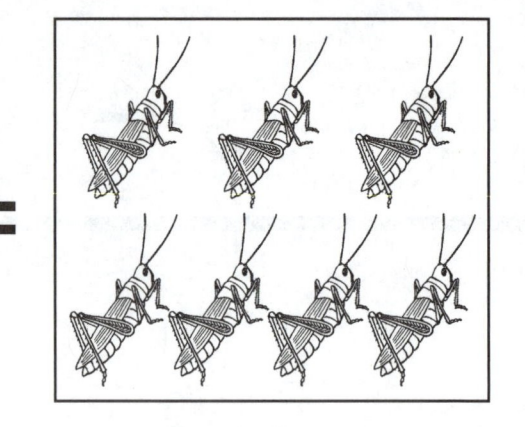

8 − 1 = ___

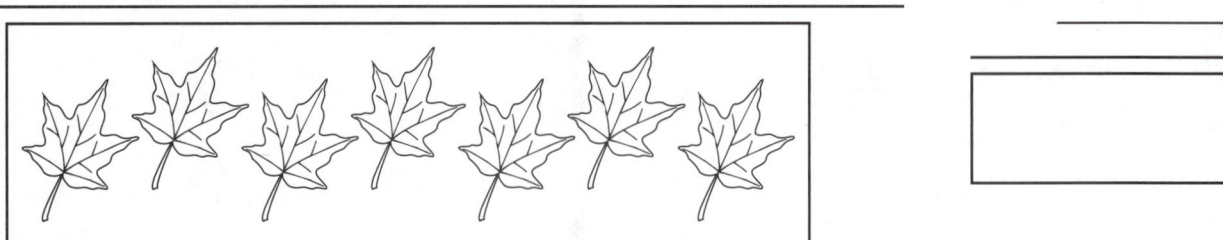

8 − 1 = ___

8 − 1 = ___

8
−1
___

8
−1
___

46   Subtract from 8

Subtract.

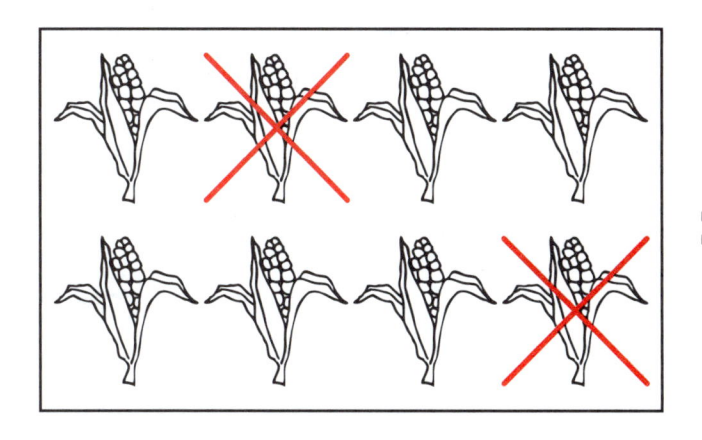

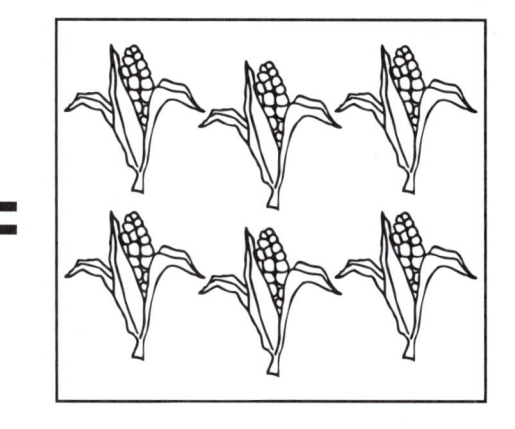

8 − 2 = ___

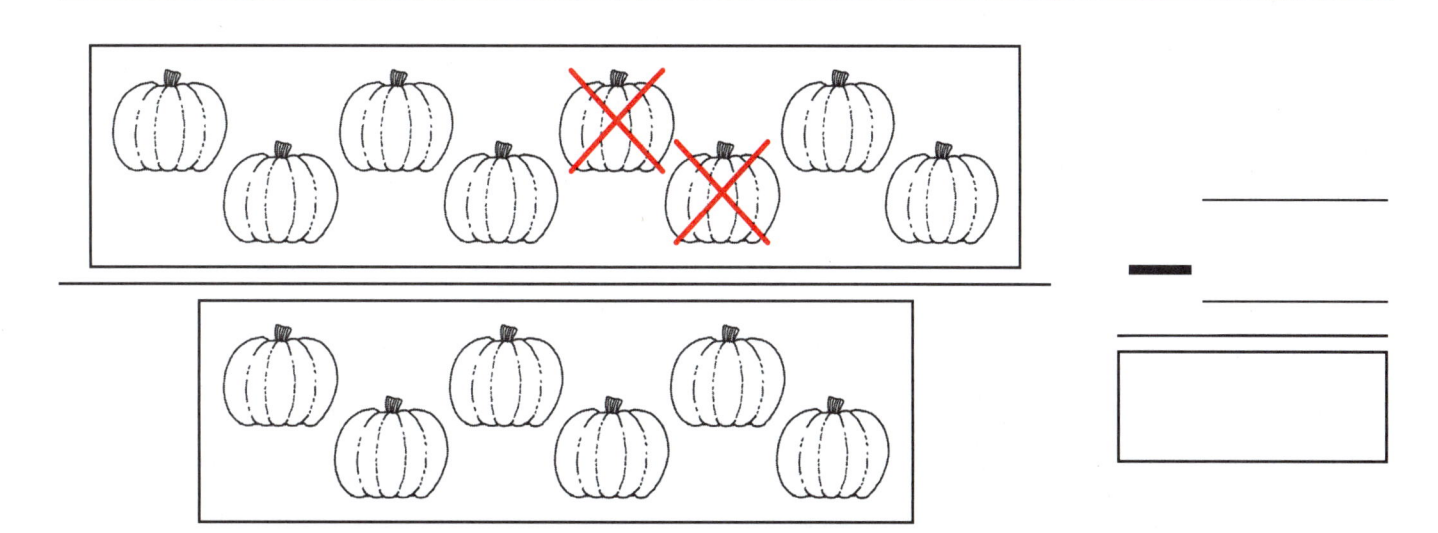

8 − 2 = ___

8 − 2 = ___

$\begin{array}{r}8\\-2\\\hline\end{array}$ $\begin{array}{r}8\\-2\\\hline\end{array}$

Subtract from 8   **47**

Subtract.

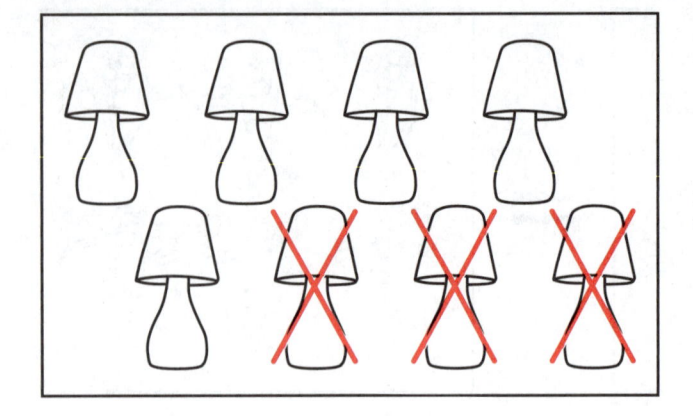

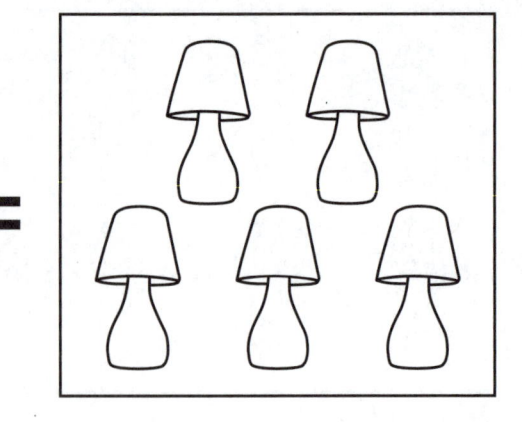

8 − 3 = ___

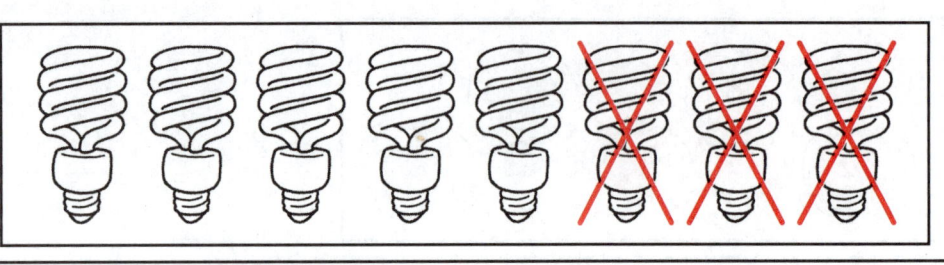

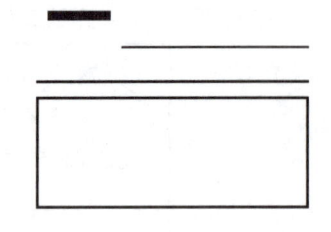

8 − 3 = ___

8 − 3 = ___

8
−3
___

8
−3
___

48 Subtract from 8

Subtract.

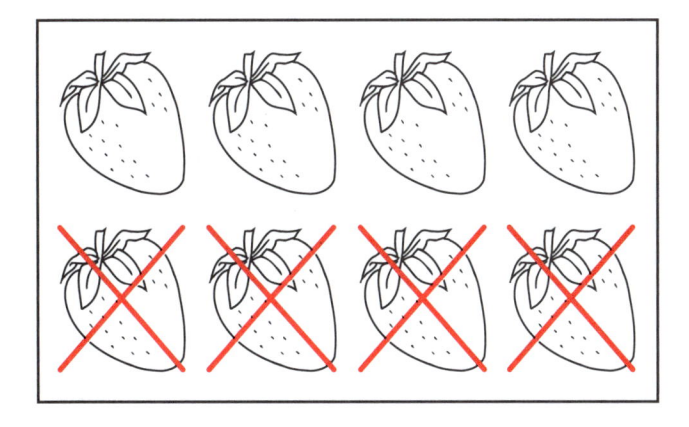

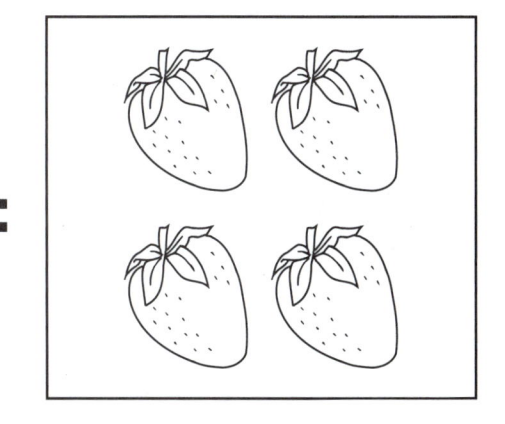

8 − 4 = ___

8 − 4 = ___

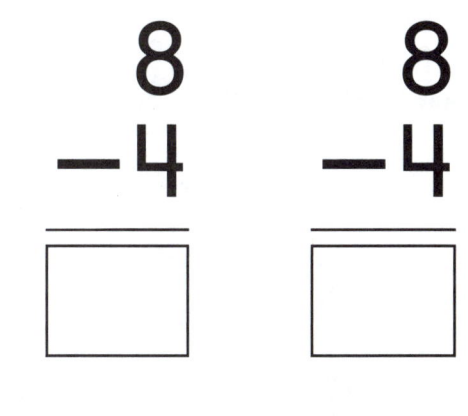

8 − 4 = ___

$\begin{array}{r}8\\-4\\\hline\end{array}$ $\begin{array}{r}8\\-4\\\hline\end{array}$

Subtract from 8   **49**

Subtract.

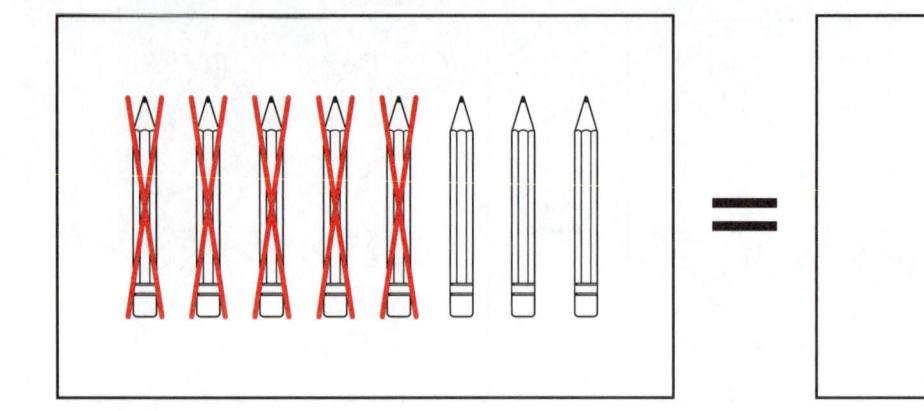

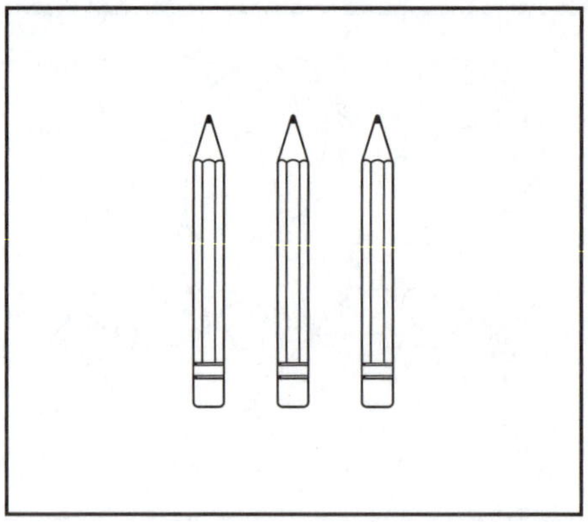

____8____ − ____5____ = ____

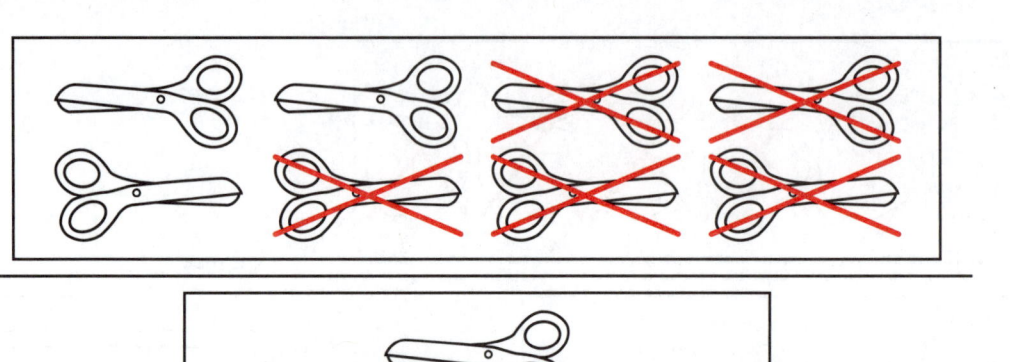

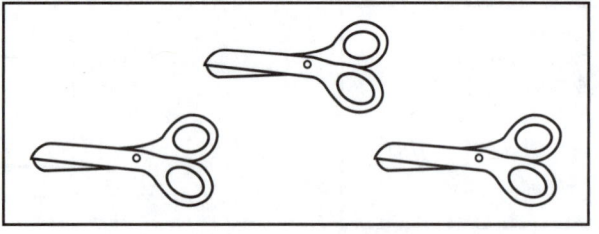

8 − 5 = ____

8 − 5 = ____

$\begin{array}{r}8\\-5\\\hline\end{array}$ $\begin{array}{r}8\\-5\\\hline\end{array}$

50   Subtract from 8

Subtract.

8 − 6 = ____

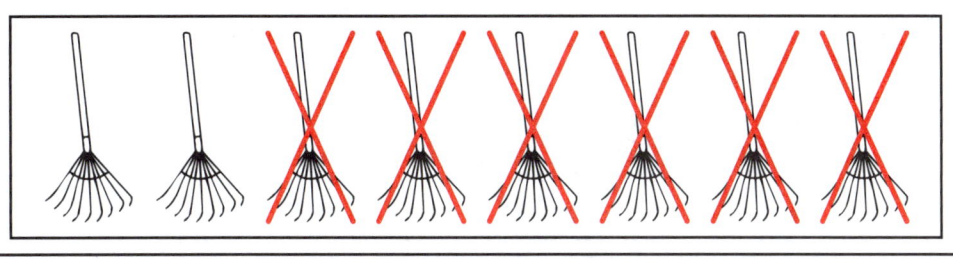

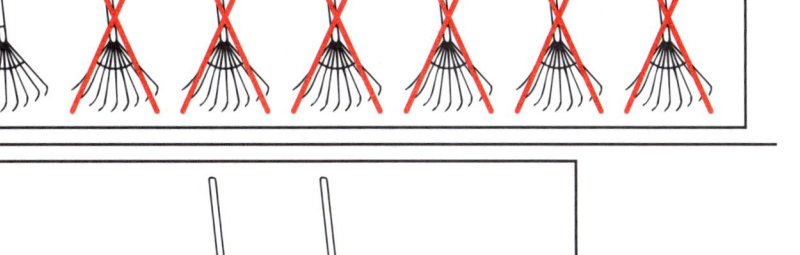

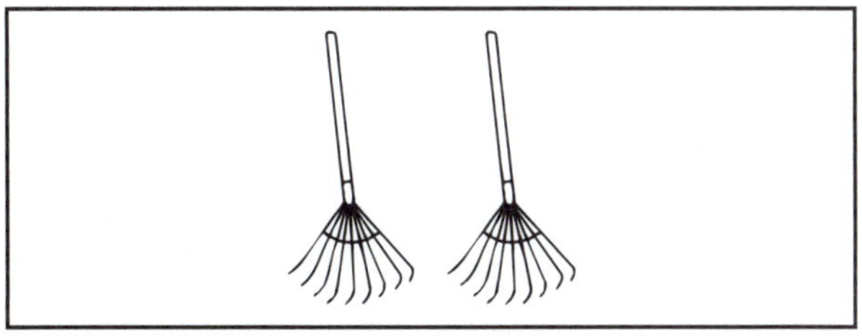

8 − 6 = ____

8 − 6 = ____

$$\begin{array}{r}8\\-6\\\hline\end{array}\qquad\begin{array}{r}8\\-6\\\hline\end{array}$$

Subtract from 8 **51**

Subtract.

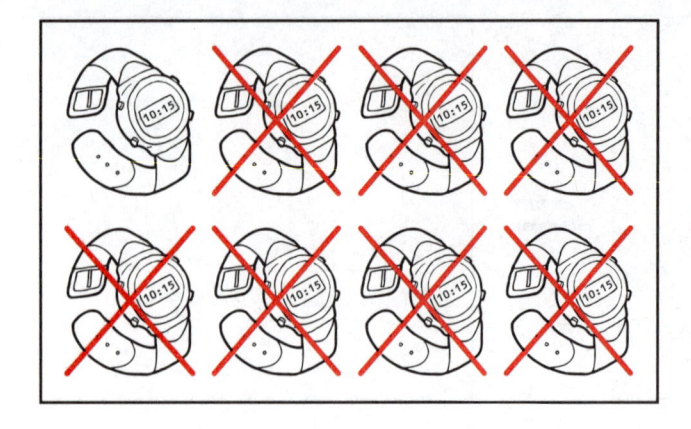

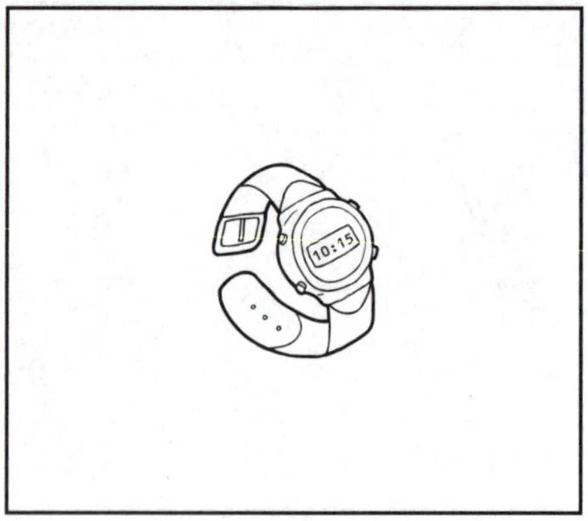

_8_ − _7_ = ___

8 − 7 = ___

8 − 7 = ___

$\begin{array}{r}8\\-7\\\hline\end{array}$ $\begin{array}{r}8\\-7\\\hline\end{array}$

52 Subtract from 8

Cross out the squares. Then write the answer.

8 − 3 =

1 − 0 =

8
−4
___

7
−5
___

8 − 1 =

8 − 5 =

8
−2
___

8
−6
___

5 − 4 =

8 − 7 =

Subtract from 1–8—Review   53

Subtract.

$3 - 0 =$

$8 - 5 =$

$$\begin{array}{r} 8 \\ -6 \\ \hline \end{array}$$

$$\begin{array}{r} 8 \\ -4 \\ \hline \end{array}$$

$1 - 1 =$

$6 - 5 =$

$$\begin{array}{r} 8 \\ -3 \\ \hline \end{array}$$

$$\begin{array}{r} 7 \\ -4 \\ \hline \end{array}$$

$5 - 4 =$

$4 - 2 =$

Subtract from 1–8 — Review

Subtract.

___9___ − ___1___ = _____

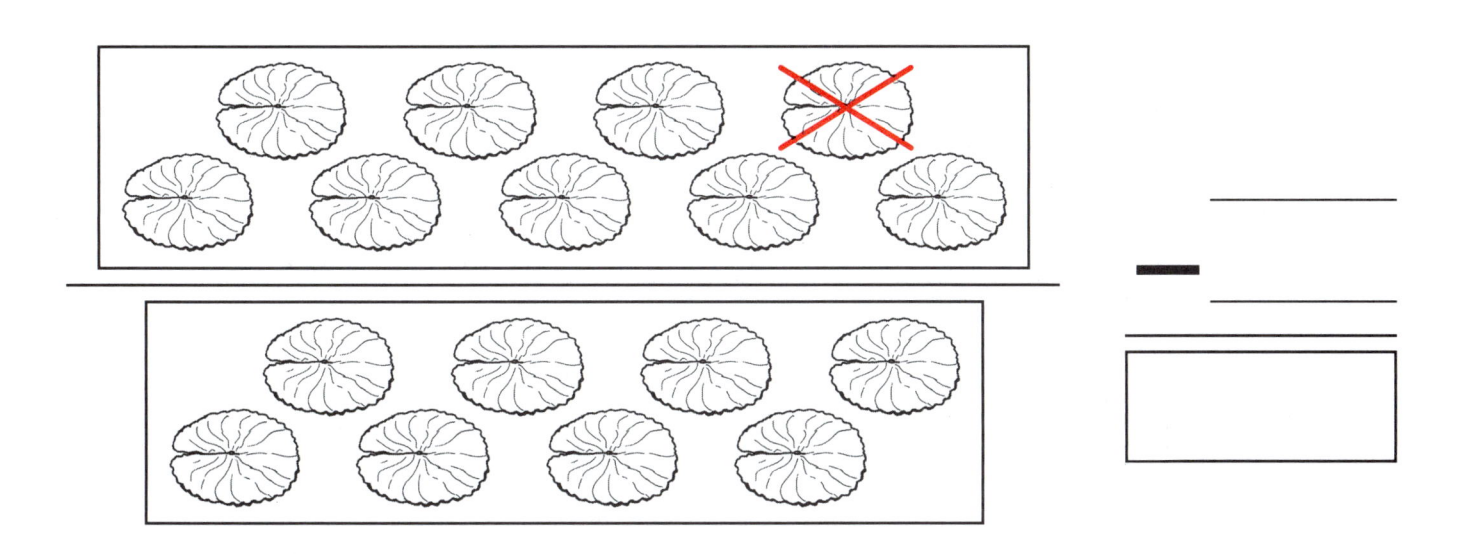

9 − 1 = _____

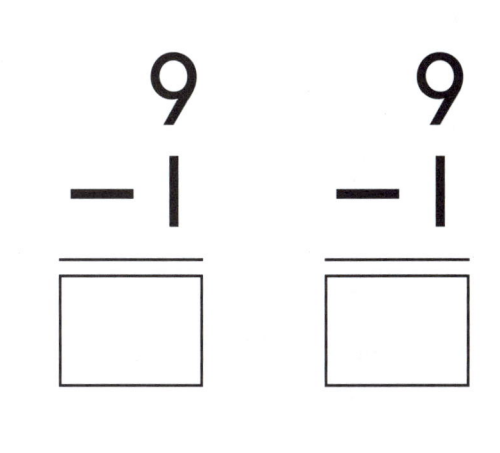

9 − 1 = _____

9
−1
___

9
−1
___

Subtract from 9 **55**

Subtract.

9 − 2 = ___

9 − 2 = ___

9 − 2 = ___

$$\begin{array}{r}9\\-2\\\hline\end{array}$$ $$\begin{array}{r}9\\-2\\\hline\end{array}$$

56   Subtract from 9

© The Continental Press, Inc.
DUPLICATING THIS MATERIAL IS ILLEGAL.

Subtract.

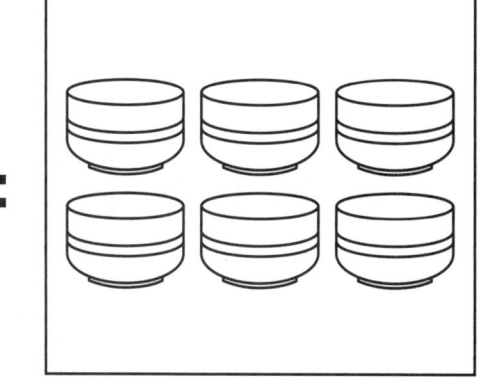

9 − 3 = ____

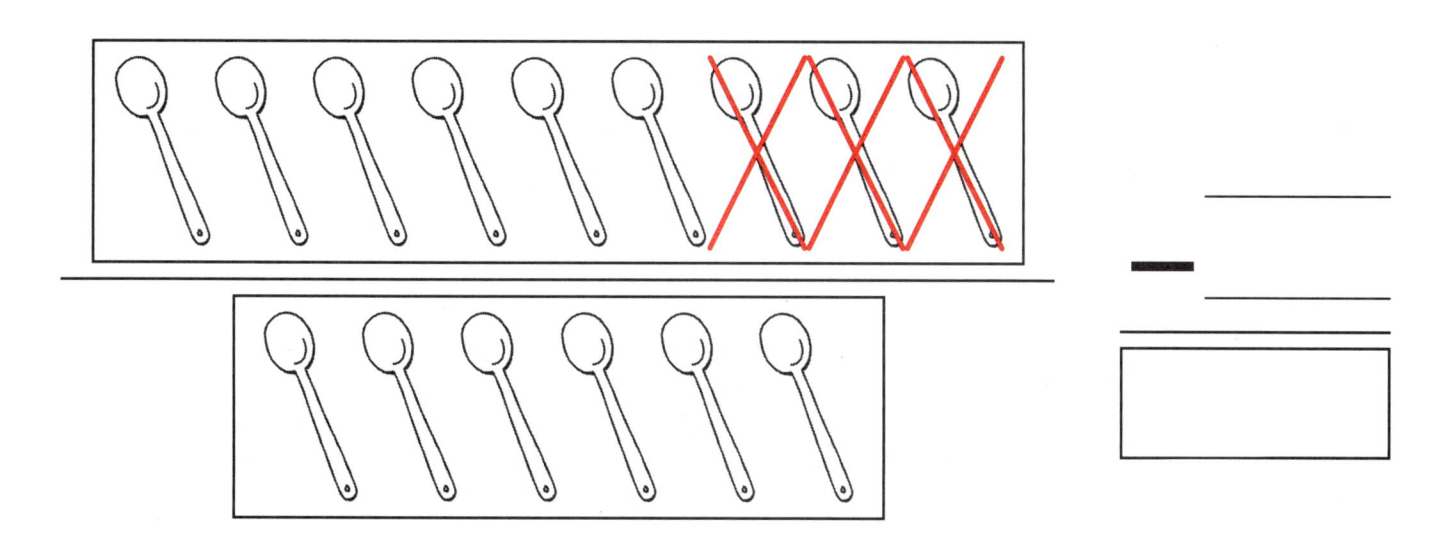

9 − 3 = ____

9 − 3 = ____

$\begin{array}{r}9\\-3\\\hline\end{array}$ $\begin{array}{r}9\\-3\\\hline\end{array}$

Subtract from 9   **57**

Subtract.

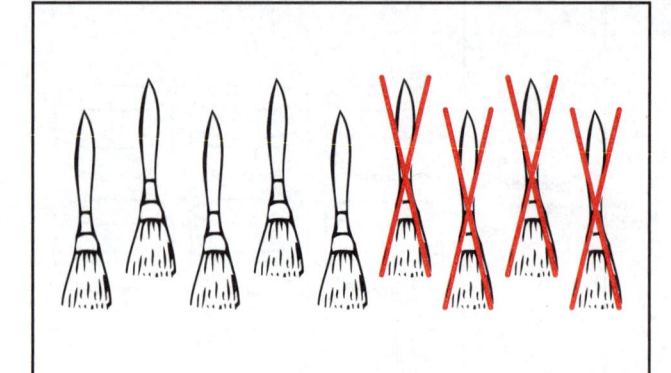

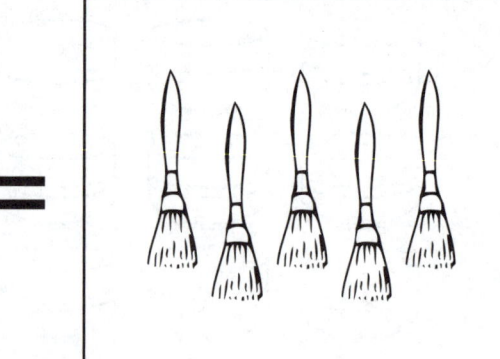

9 − 4 = ___

9 − 4 = ___

9 − 4 = ___

$\begin{array}{r}9\\-4\\\hline\end{array}$ $\begin{array}{r}9\\-4\\\hline\end{array}$

58   Subtract from 9

Subtract.

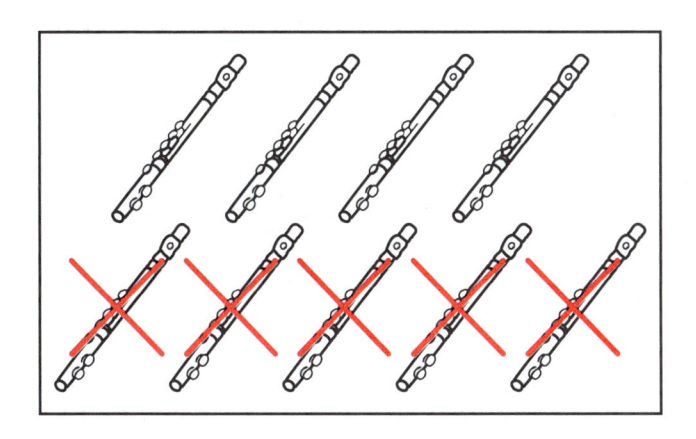

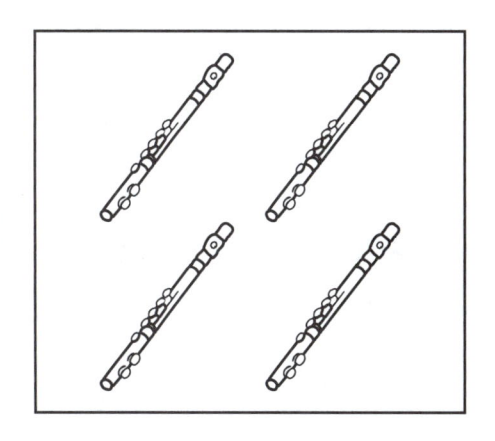

9 − 5 = ___

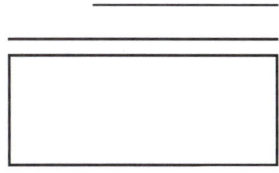

9 − 5 = ___

9 − 5 = ___

9 − 5 = ___

$\begin{array}{r}9\\-5\\\hline\end{array}$ $\begin{array}{r}9\\-5\\\hline\end{array}$

Subtract from 9

Subtract.

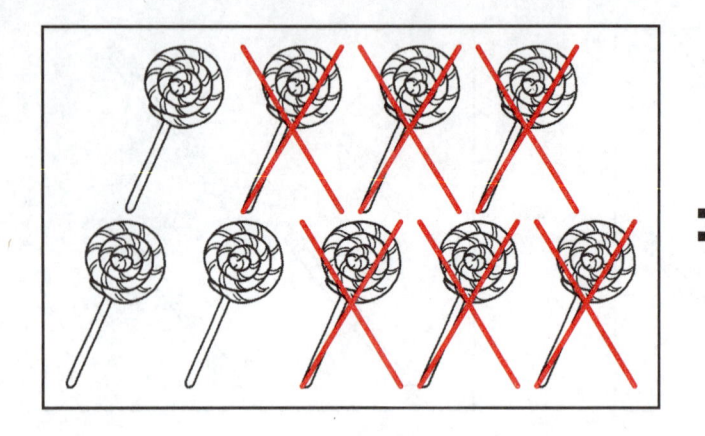

_9_ − _6_ = ____

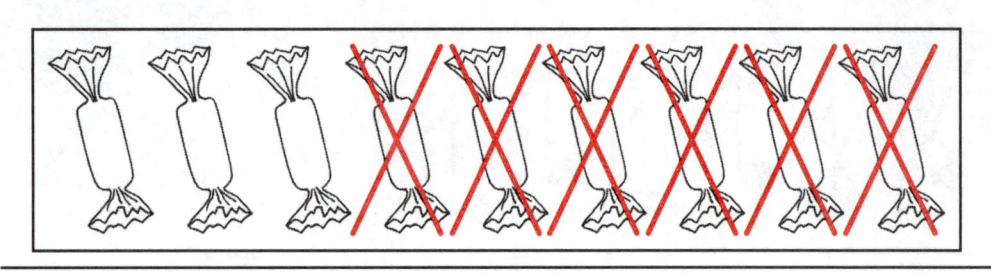

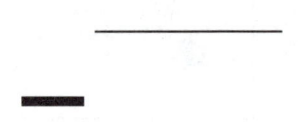

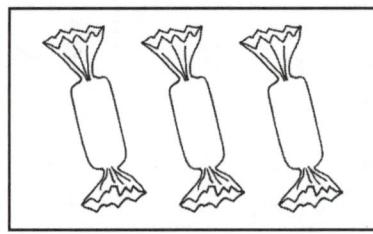

9 − 6 = ____

9 − 6 = ____

$$\begin{array}{r}9\\-6\\\hline\end{array}$$ $$\begin{array}{r}9\\-6\\\hline\end{array}$$

Subtract from 9

Subtract.

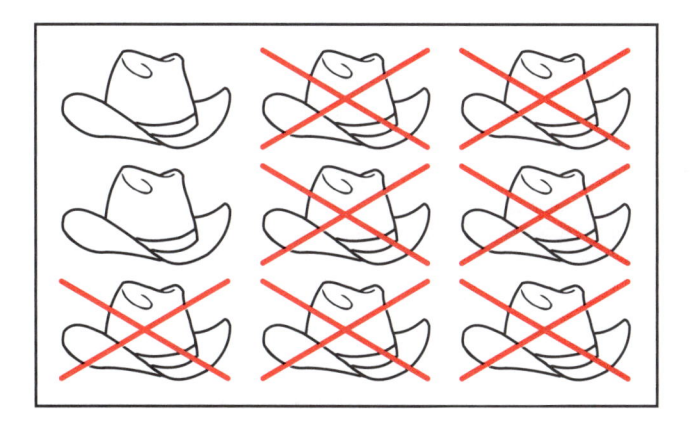

9 − 7 = ___

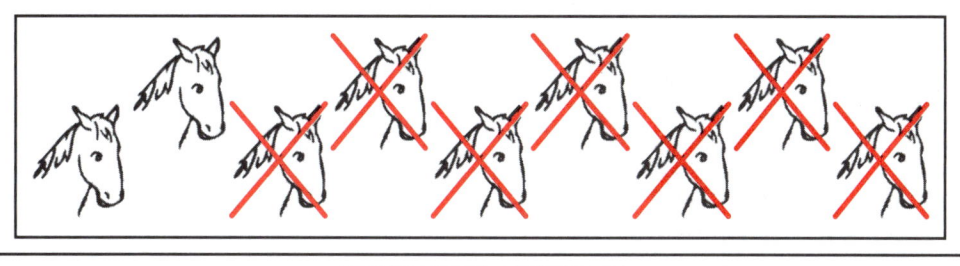

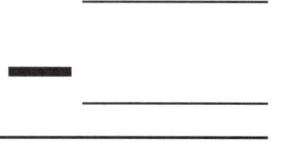

9 − 7 = ___

9 − 7 = ___

9
−7
___

9
−7
___

Subtract from 9 **61**

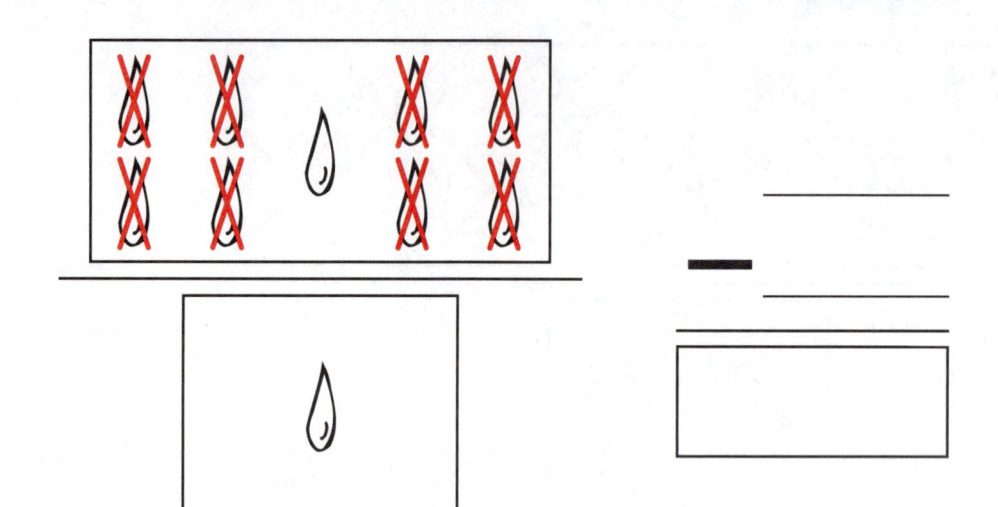

Subtract.

9 − 8 = ___

9 − 8 = ___

9 − 8 = ___

$\begin{array}{r}9\\-8\\\hline\end{array}$ $\begin{array}{r}9\\-8\\\hline\end{array}$

62 Subtract from 9

Cross out the squares.
Then write the answer.

9 − 4 =

9 − 7 =

9
−8

9
−3

1 − 0 =

7 − 5 =

5
−4

9
−6

9 − 5 =

9 − 2 =

Subtract from 1–9—Review **63**

Subtract.

5 − 2 =

9 − 6 =

4
$\underline{-0}$

9
$\underline{-4}$

9 − 8 =

6 − 4 =

9
$\underline{-2}$

7
$\underline{-3}$

1 − 1 =

8 − 5 =

Word problems tell a number story. Then they ask a question about the story. You have to use your math skills to answer the question. Read the story. Then decide how to find the answer.

Write the problem with numbers. Sometimes you can draw pictures to help you. Then write the answer.

Look at the word problem below. The picture helps you find the answer.

There are 2 🐰.
1 🐰 hops away.
How many 🐰 are left?

$$2 - 1 = 1$$

Read each story. Subtract.

Rosa has 3 🍭.
She eats 2 🍭.
How many 🍭 are left?

Ben has 6 ⚾.
3 ⚾ get lost.
How many ⚾ are left?

Word Problems—Teaching Page

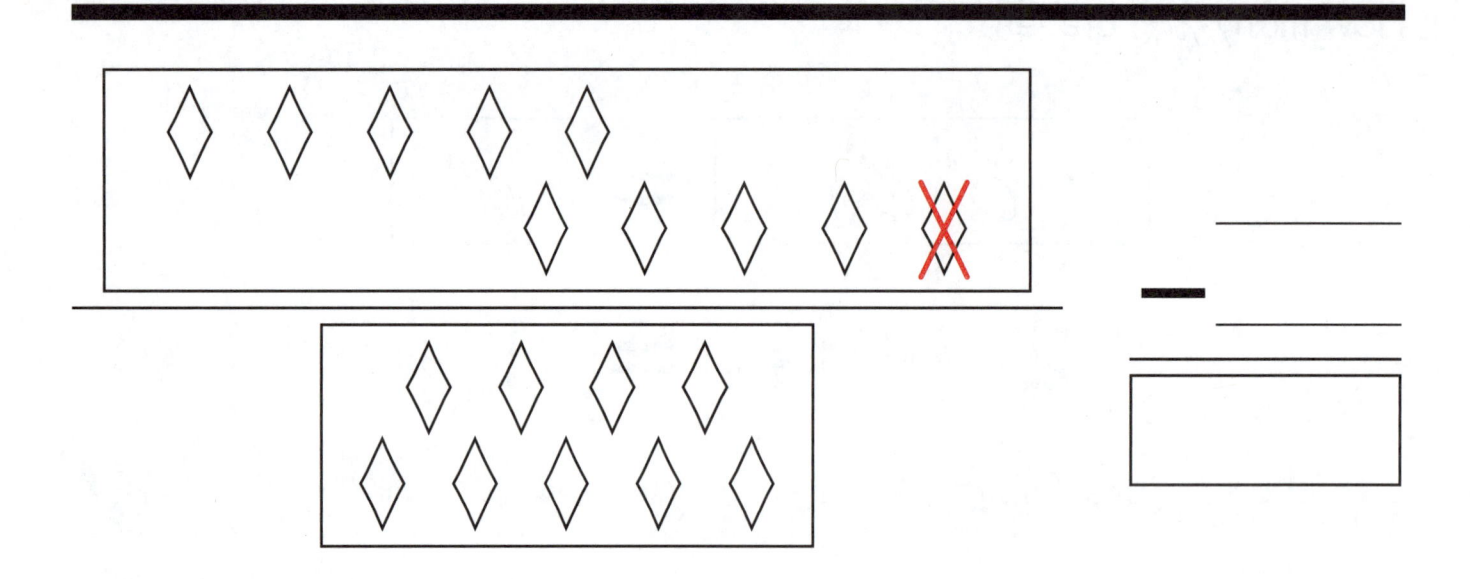

Subtract.

10 - 1 = ___

10 - 1 = ___

10 - 1 = ___

       10   10
     − 1   − 1

66   Subtract from 10

Subtract.

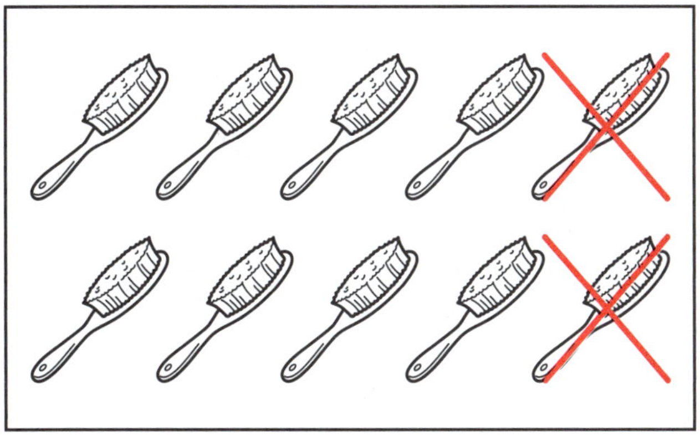

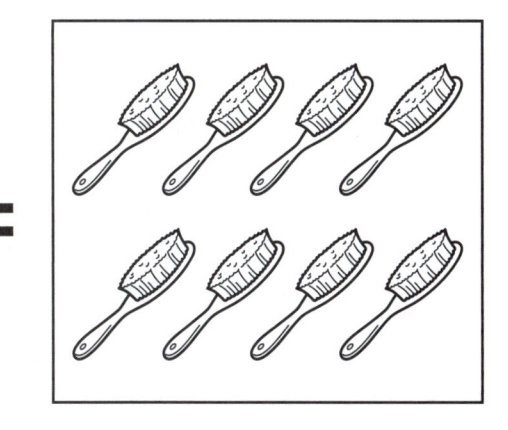

10 − 2 = ___

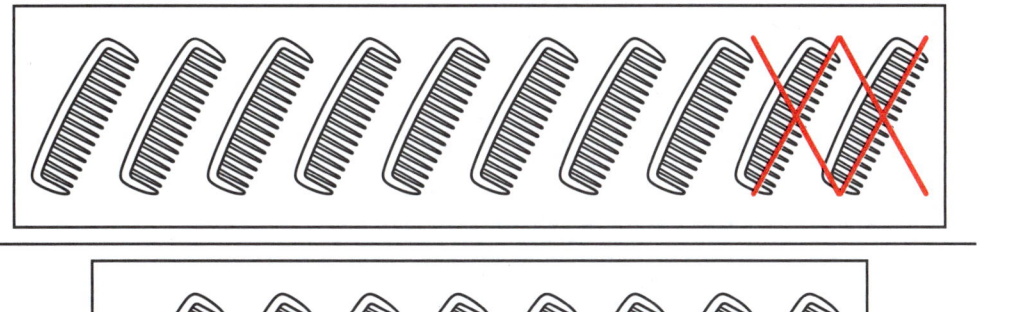

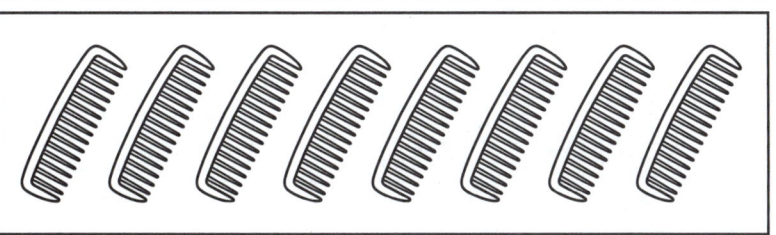

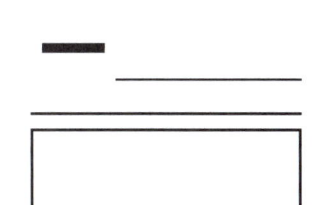

10 − 2 = ___

10 − 2 = ___

10
− 2
____

10
− 2
____

Subtract from 10 **67**

Subtract.

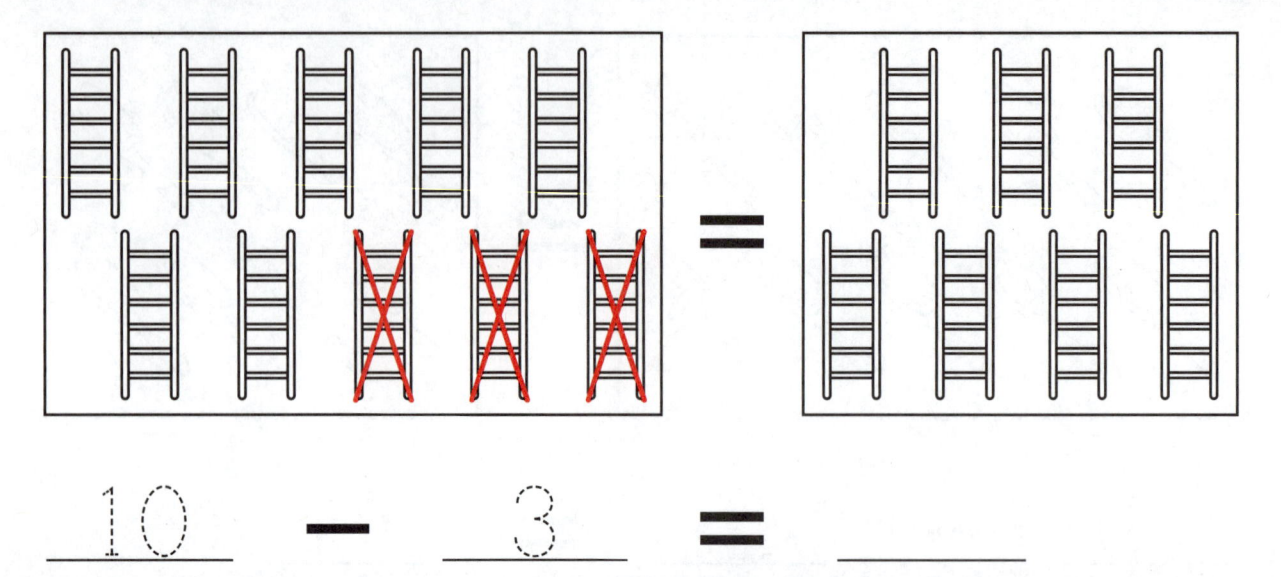

__10__ − __3__ = ____

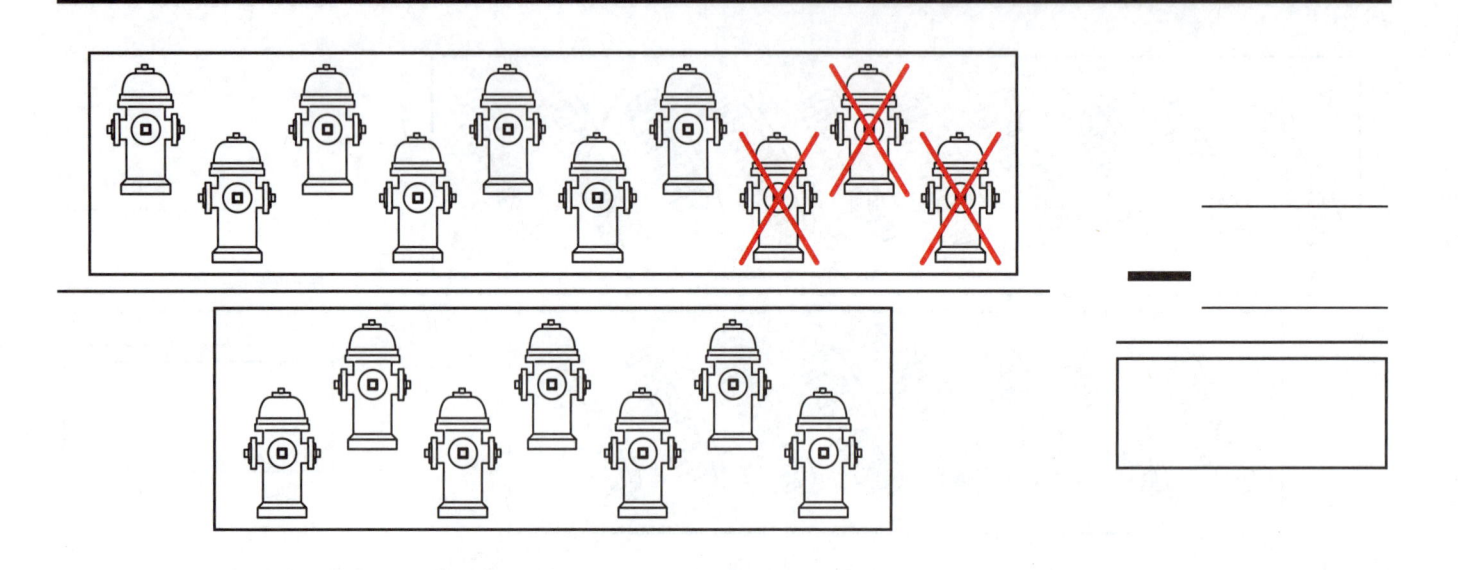

10 − 3 = ____

10 − 3 = ____

  10
− 3
_____

  10
− 3
_____

68   Subtract from 10

Subtract.

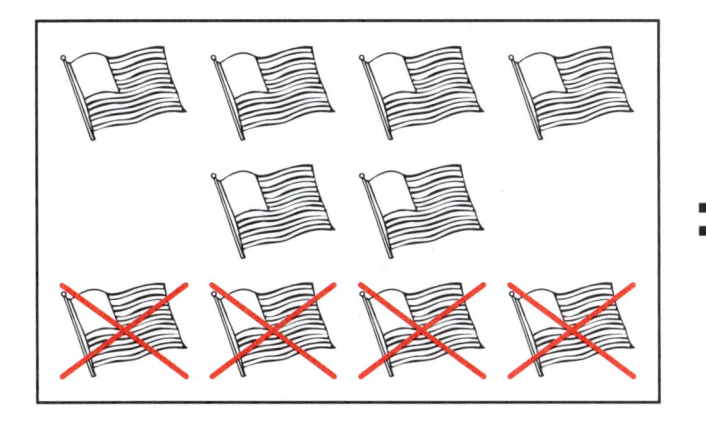

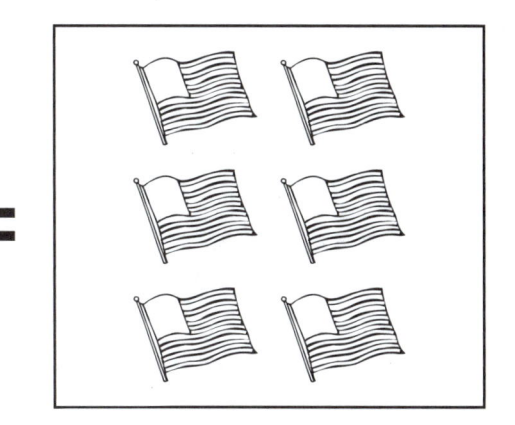

10 − 4 = ____

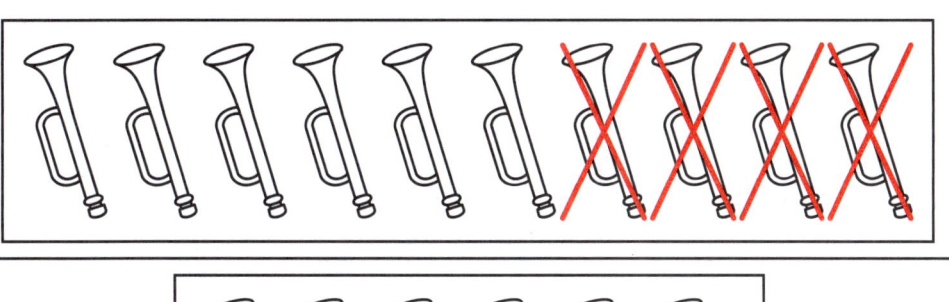

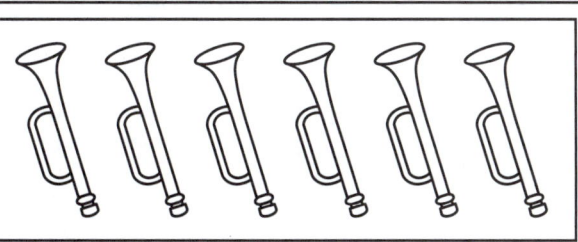

10 − 4 = ____

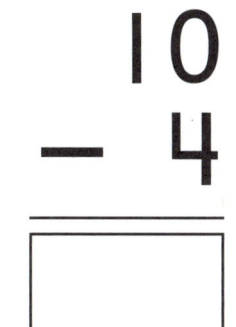

10 − 4 = ____

10
− 4
____

10
− 4
____

Subtract from 10   **69**

Subtract.

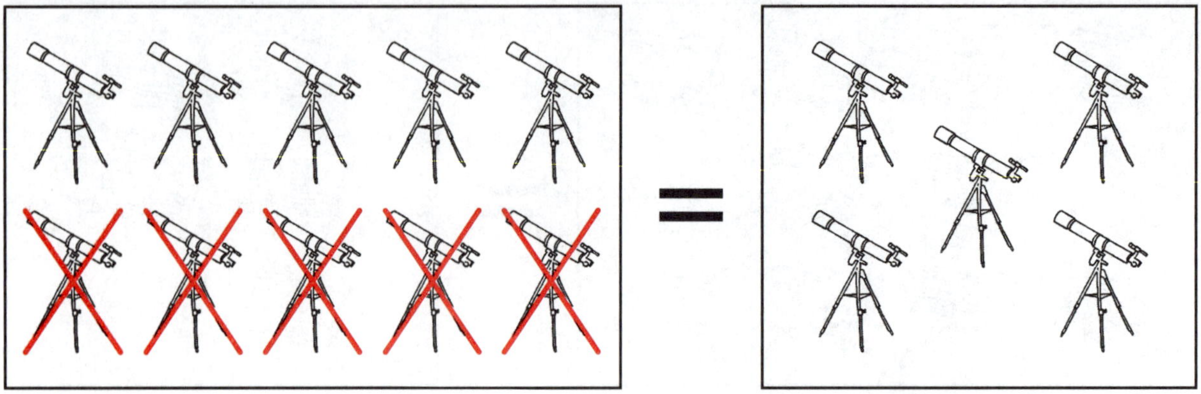

10 - 5 = ___

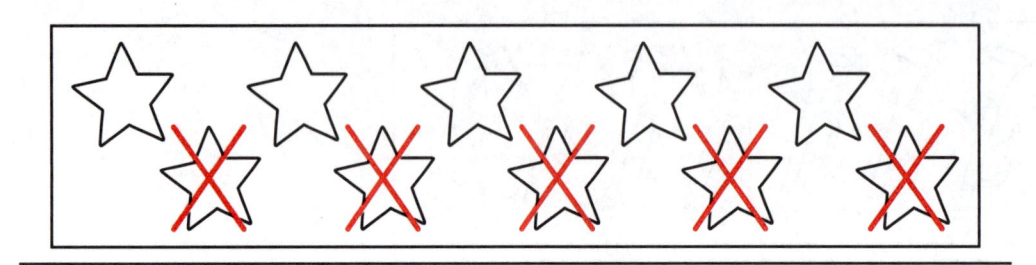

10 - 5 = ___

10 - 5 = ___

10
− 5
___

10
− 5
___

70 Subtract from 10

Subtract.

10 − 6 = ____

10 − 6 = ____

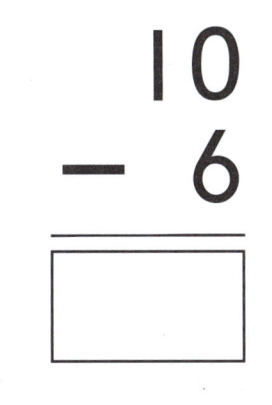

10 − 6 = ____

$$\begin{array}{r} 10 \\ -6 \\ \hline \end{array}$$

$$\begin{array}{r} 10 \\ -6 \\ \hline \end{array}$$

Subtract from 10 **71**

© The Continental Press, Inc.
DUPLICATING THIS MATERIAL IS ILLEGAL.

Subtract.

10 − 7 = ___

10 − 7 = ___

10 − 7 = ___

$$\begin{array}{r} 10 \\ -7 \\ \hline \end{array}$$
$$\begin{array}{r} 10 \\ -7 \\ \hline \end{array}$$

72   Subtract from 10

Subtract.

__10__ − __8__ = ____

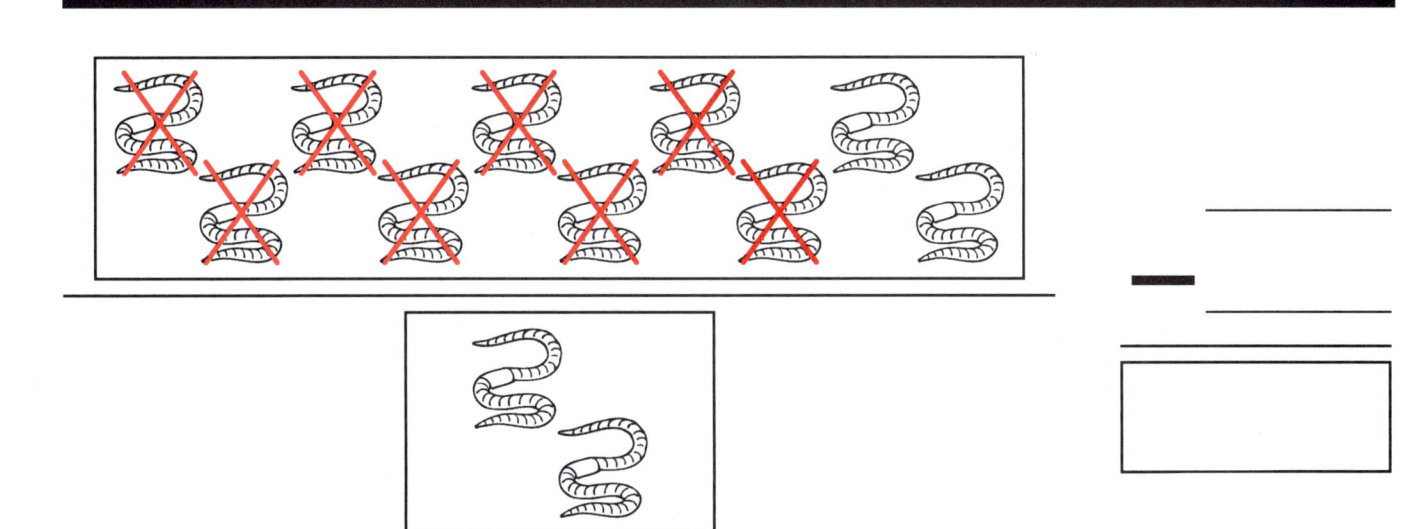

10 − 8 = ____

10 − 8 = ____

 10
− 8
____

 10
− 8
____

Subtract from 10   **73**

Subtract.

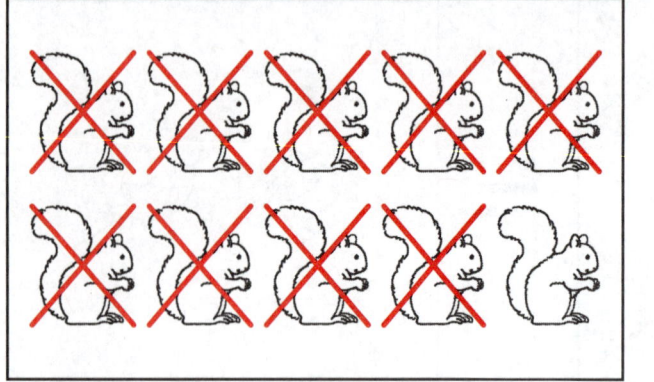

___10___ − ___9___ = _____

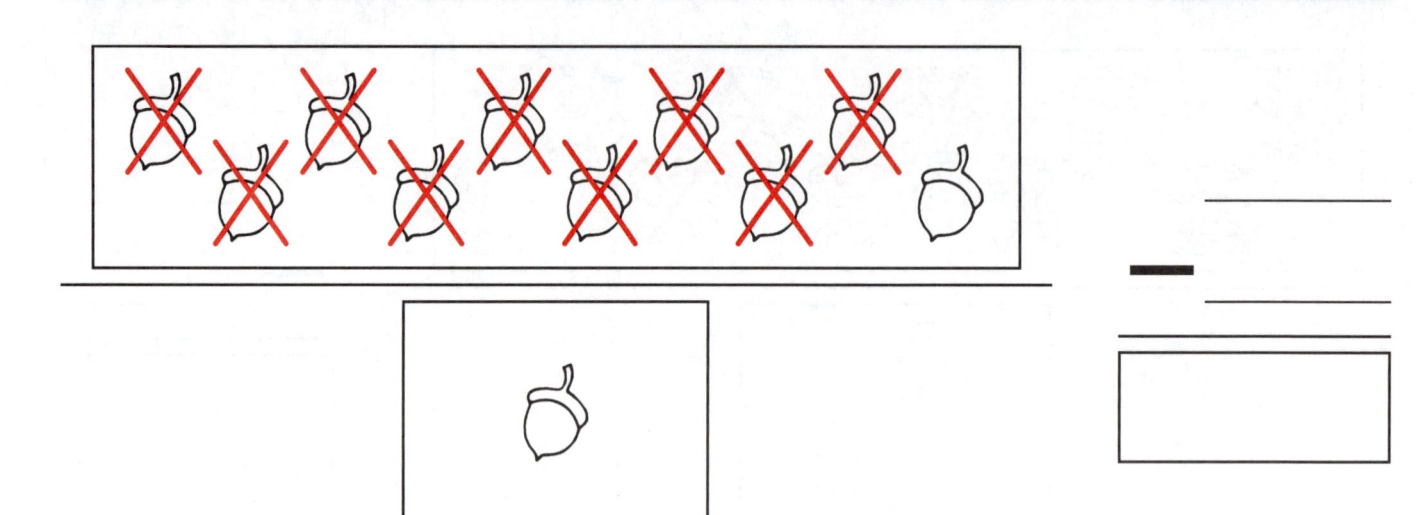

10 − 9 = _____

10 − 9 = _____

  10   10
− 9   − 9
____   ____

74 Subtract from 10

**Cross out the squares.
Then write the answer.**

10 − 6 =

10 − 2 =

10
− 3

4
−4

1 − 0 =

10 − 1 =

10
− 4

10
− 8

10 − 9 =

10 − 7 =

Subtract from 1–10—Review   **75**

Subtract.

1 − 1 =

9 − 8 =

9
-3
___

10
-7
___

10 − 6 =

8 − 2 =

8
-6
___

6
-5
___

4 − 0 =

10 − 5 =

76 Subtract from 1–10—Review

Read each story. Subtract.

There are 8 🐸.
3 🐸 hop away.
How many 🐸 are left?

Lee has 10 🍦. 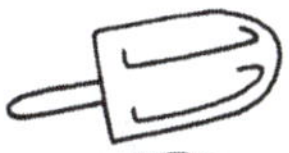
He eats 8 🍦. 
How many 🍦 are left?

Pam has 4 🌼.
She gives 2 🌼 away.
How many 🌼 are left?

Sally has 9 ✏️. 
5 ✏️ break.
How many ✏️ are left?

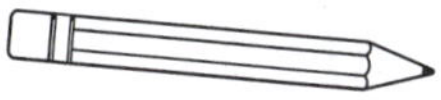

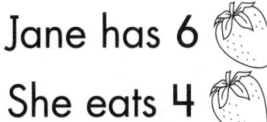

Jane has 6 🍓.
She eats 4 🍓.
How many 🍓 are left?

José has 3 🐕. 
He gives 1 🐕 away.
How many 🐕 are left?

Word Problems

Subtract.

___6___ − ___6___ = _____

6 − 6 = _____

6 − 6 = _____

$$\begin{array}{r}6\\-6\\\hline\end{array}$$ $$\begin{array}{r}6\\-6\\\hline\end{array}$$

78 Subtract Equal Numbers

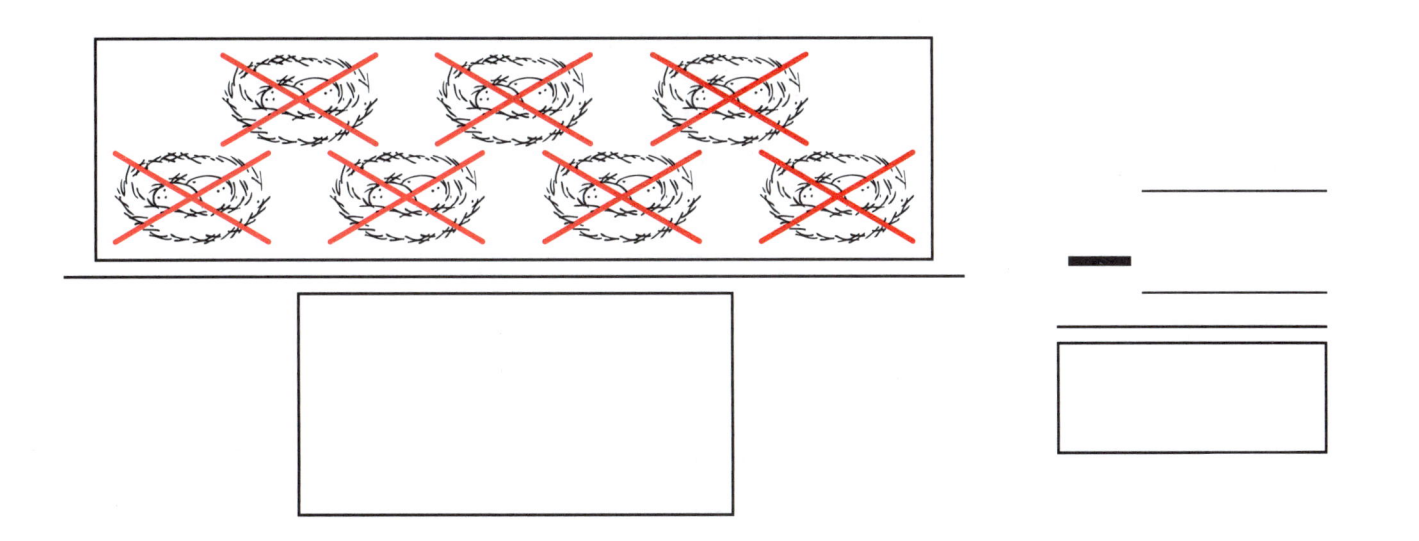

Subtract.

7 − 7 = ___

7 − 7 = ___

7 − 7 = ___

7
−7
___

7
−7
___

Subtract Equal Numbers **79**

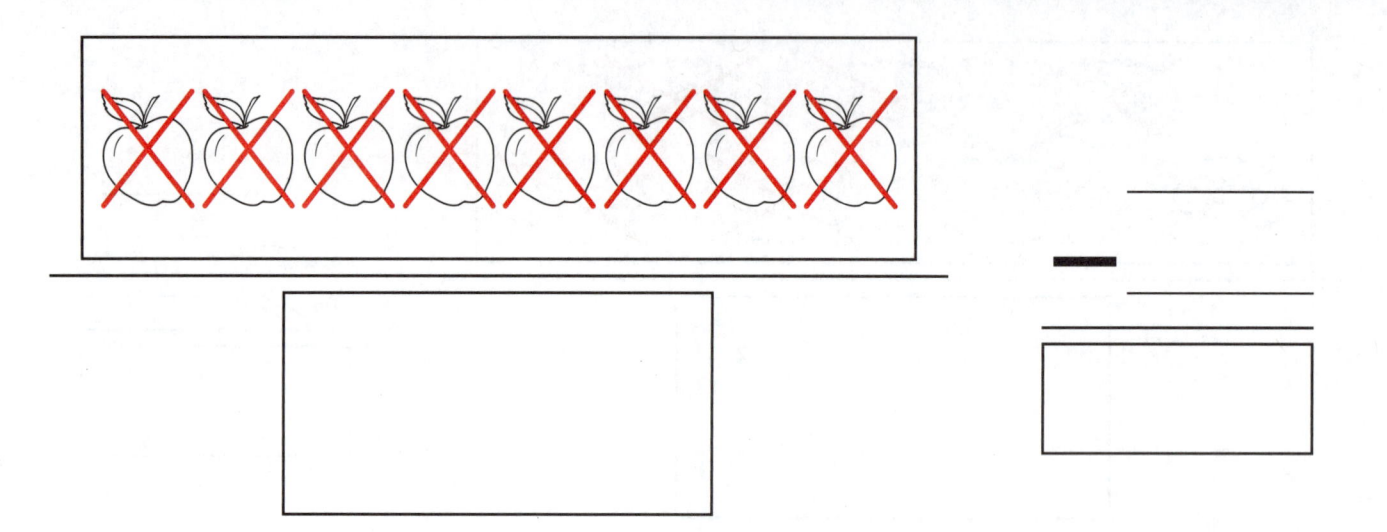

Subtract.

___8___ − ___8___ = _____

8 − 8 = _____

8 − 8 = _____

$\begin{array}{r}8\\-8\\\hline\end{array}$ $\begin{array}{r}8\\-8\\\hline\end{array}$

80 Subtract Equal Numbers

Subtract.

____9____ − ____9____ = _____

9 − 9 = _____

9 − 9 = _____

  9
−9
___

  9
−9
___

Subtract Equal Numbers **81**

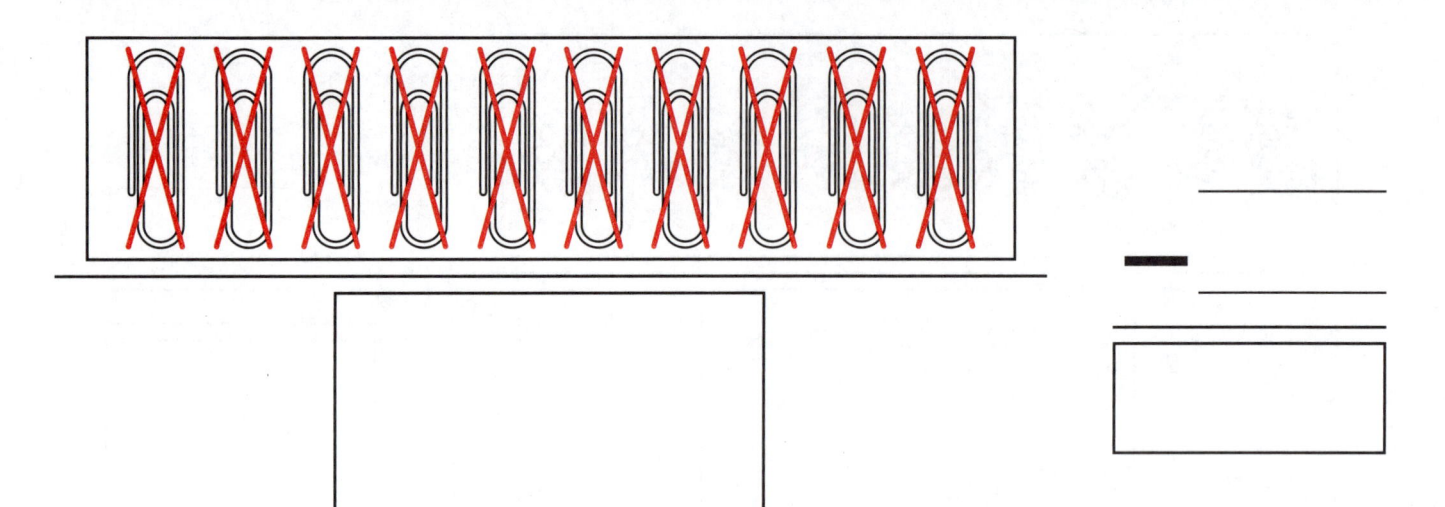

Subtract.

___10___ − ___10___ = _____

10 − 10 = _____

10 − 10 = _____

  10   10
−10   −10

82 Subtract Equal Numbers

Subtract.

6 − 0 = ____

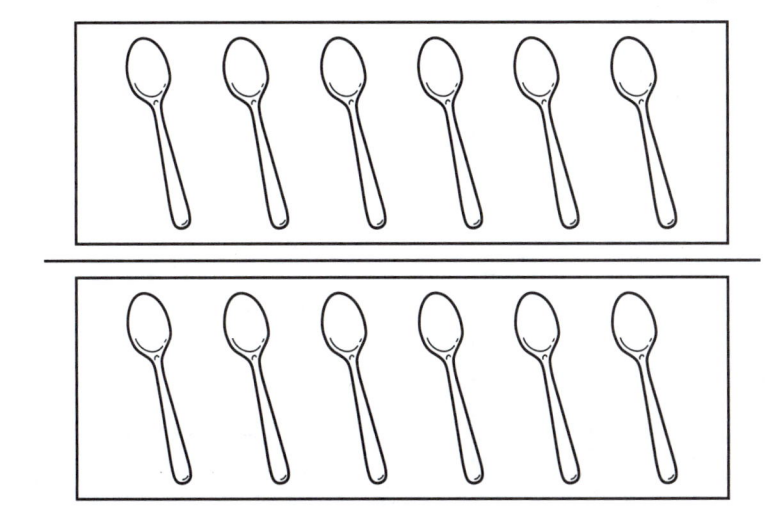

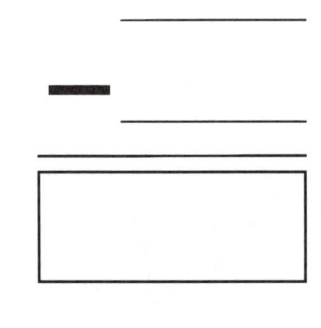

6 − 0 = ____

6 − 0 = ____

| 6 | 6 |
| −0 | −0 |

Subtract 0 **83**

Subtract.

7 − 0 = ____

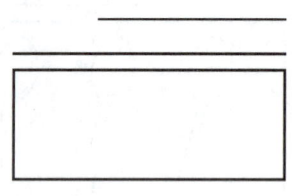

7 − 0 = ____

7 − 0 = ____

| 7
− 0
____

   7
− 0
____

84 Subtract 0

Subtract.

8 − 0 = ____

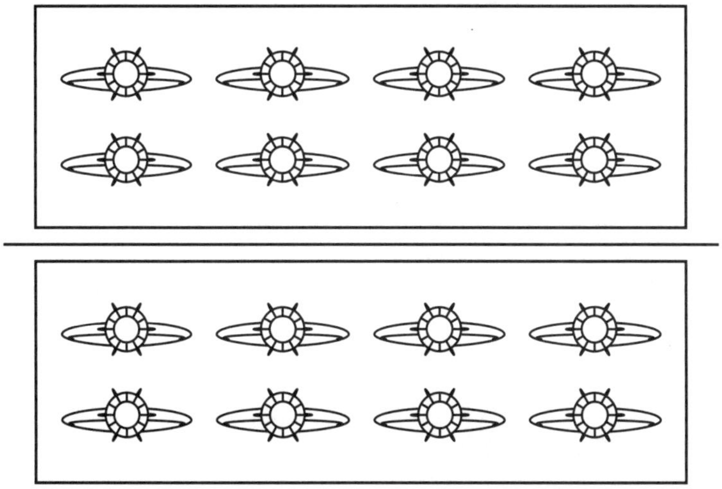

8 − 0 = ____

8 − 0 = ____

8   8
−0 −0

Subtract 0   **85**

Subtract.

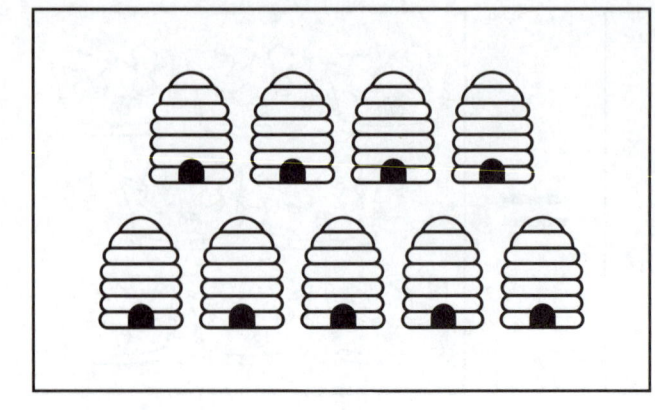

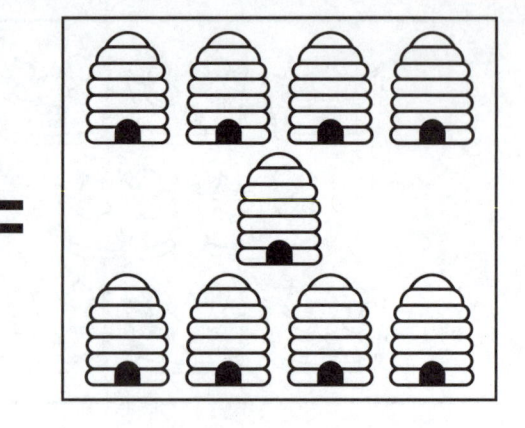

9 − 0 = ___

___ − ___ = ▢

9 − 0 = ___

9 − 0 = ___

9
−0
___

9
−0
___

86 Subtract 0

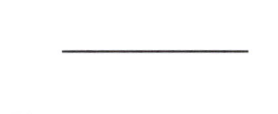

Subtract.

10 − 0 = ___

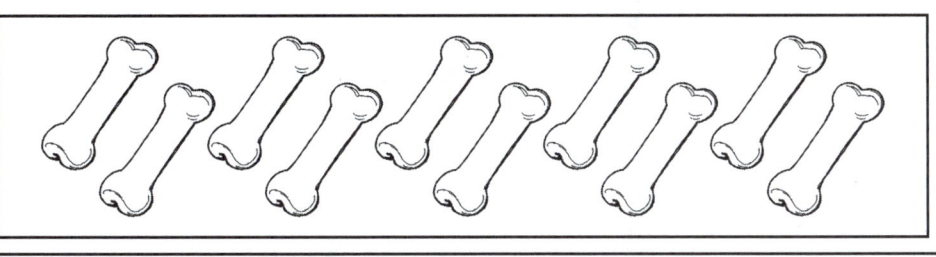

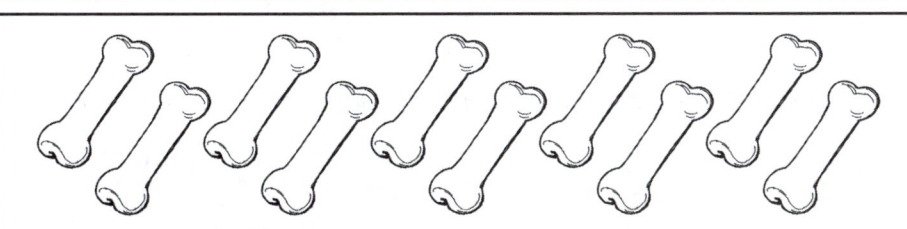

10 − 0 = ___

10 − 0 = ___

   10   10
− 0   − 0

Subtract 0   **87**

**Cross out the squares.
Then write the answer.**

6 − 6 =

10 − 0 =

6
−0
___

10
− 4
___

8 − 0 =

9 − 9 =

9
−0
___

8
−8
___

10 − 10 =

9 − 2 =

88 Subtract 0–10—Review

Subtract.

$6 - 1 =$	$7 - 7 =$
7 -0	6 -4
$9 - 9 =$	$8 - 5 =$
9 -6	9 -0
$7 - 3 =$	$10 - 10 =$

Cross out the squares. Then write the answer.

9 − 7 =

10 − 10 =

10
− 9
___

3
−0
___

7 − 7 =

5 − 2 =

8
−4
___

6
−3
___

8 − 3 =

9 − 4 =

90   Subtract 0–10—Review

Subtract.

$10 - 10 =$	$7 - 0 =$
$\begin{array}{r} 8 \\ -1 \\ \hline \end{array}$	$\begin{array}{r} 10 \\ -7 \\ \hline \end{array}$
$8 - 6 =$	$9 - 5 =$
$\begin{array}{r} 7 \\ -5 \\ \hline \end{array}$	$\begin{array}{r} 9 \\ -3 \\ \hline \end{array}$
$6 - 2 =$	$4 - 4 =$

Subtract 0–10—Review

Read each story. Subtract.

Kelly sees 5 🕊.
2 🕊 fly away.
How many 🕊 are left?

Jim has 8 🧁.
He sells 6 🧁.
How many 🧁 are left?

Tom has 7 ⭐.
He loses 2 ⭐.
How many ⭐ are left?

Pat has 3 🍐.
She eats 3 🍐.
How many 🍐 are left?

Kim has 6 📕.
She gives 5 📕 away.
How many 📕 are left?

There are 10 🕷.
6 🕷 run away.
How many 🕷 are left?

92   Word Problems

Draw and write the answer.

3 take away 1 = ___

Subtract.

$$\begin{array}{r}4\\-2\\\hline\end{array}$$

5 − 3 = ___

$$\begin{array}{r}3\\-1\\\hline\end{array}$$

Read the story. Subtract.

Maria has 5 🎵.
4 🎵 break.
How many 🎵 are left?

Pretest/Posttest **T-1**

Subtract.

$$5 - 0 =$$

$$9 - 4 =$$

$$6 - 6 =$$

$$10 - 6 =$$

$$8 - 5 =$$

$$7 - 2 =$$

Read the story. Subtract.

There are 7 🐝.
Then 4 🐝 fly away.
How many 🐝 are left?

T-2   Pretest/Posttest

Draw and write the answer.

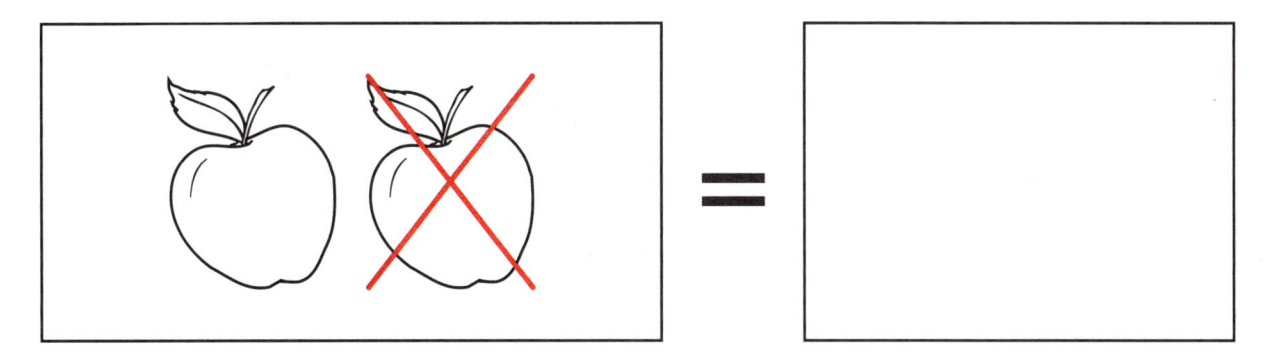

2 take away 1 = _____

Subtract.

5
−2
___

3 − 2 = _____

4
−1
___

Read the story. Subtract.

Dan has 5 shells.
He gives 3 shells away.
How many shells are left?

Pretest/Posttest **T-3**

Subtract.

$$7 - 0$$

$$8 - 4$$

$$6 - 5$$

$$9 - 3$$

$$10 - 7 =$$

$$4 - 4 =$$

Read the story. Subtract.

A dog has 10 🦴.
It eats 2 🦴.
How many 🦴 are left?

T-4   Pretest/Posttest